FORBIDDEN HISTORY
BURIED REALMS

The Myths, Legends, and Subterranean Worlds
That Mainstream History Refuses to Explain

ZACK D. HISTORY

FORBIDDEN HISTORY

Table of Contents

Introduction: The Doors Beneath Our Feet 4

Part I: Legends of the Hollow Earth 18

Chapter 1: The Hollow Earth Hypothesis 18

Chapter 2: Shambhala and Agartha 33

Chapter 3: Hell, Hades, and the Underworld 48

Part II: Subterranean Cities and Lost Civilizations 65

Chapter 4: The World Below Cappadocia 65

Chapter 5: The Labyrinths of Egypt 80

Chapter 6: The Caves of the Americas 96

Part III: Myths, Monsters, and Forbidden Knowledge 109

Chapter 7: The Guardians of the Deep 109

Chapter 8: The Suppression of Subterranean Lore 120

Chapter 9: Caves as Gateways to Other Realities 139

Part IV: Patterns and Possibilities 152

Chapter 10: The Archetypal Underground Journey 152

Chapter 11: Science Meets Myth 168

Chapter 12: Why the Buried Realms Matter 185

Bonus Section: Buried Realms Workbook 208

Conclusion 237

Introduction

The Doors Beneath Our Feet

What if the greatest secrets of our past are not written in the stars, but buried beneath our feet?

That is where the old stories send us—downward. Not up to heavens peopled with distant gods, but into the earth itself: through volcanic throats and limestone veins, into black halls where whispers carry, where light is a trespass and time sifts like dust. The world's folklore is obsessed with entrances: sinkholes that swallow armies, wells that speak, trapdoors under temples, labyrinths threaded beneath palaces, and pilgrim paths that descend into the bone-chilling darkness. There are the legendary hollows of the Earth; the luminous cities of Shambhala and Agartha; tunnels rumoured beneath pyramids and stupas; catacombs and serpent-guarded gates; sanctuaries carved into mountains; and entire subterranean towns hidden from history's official gaze.

The mainstream posture is familiar: "myth," "metaphor," "misunderstanding." And yet – we keep finding doors. No one denies the multilevel underground cities of Cappadocia cut into tuff and linked by stone-rolled portals; or the vast karst cave systems that lace the Americas; or the ritual chambers and engineered passages discovered beneath ancient ceremonial centers on several continents. When so many cultures, separated by oceans and centuries, tell versions of the same story—a below-world that matters—perhaps the responsible response is not dismissal but inquiry.

This book is that inquiry.

Why Myths of Hidden Worlds Persist Across Cultures

Myth is not the opposite of truth; it's one of truth's oldest dialects. Myths endure when they crystallize experiences too deep, too strange, or too sacred to be pinned by ledger and law. The below-world recurs because it solves multiple problems—spiritual, psychological, and practical—at once.

First, the subterranean as a sanctuary and technology. In harsh climates and volatile eras, rock is a dependable ally. Nature offers shelter, storage, water capture, defensive choke points, and stable temperatures underground. Communities that learned to bend the earth to their purposes survived droughts and raids that others did not. People remember—first as practice, later as a story.

Second, the subterranean is a classroom for the mind. In absolute darkness, the brain projects. Rhythms slow; perception narrows; small sounds expand. Drumming resonates differently. Breathing becomes landscape. Whether fasting, chanting, or ingesting ritual sacraments, humans have long used caves and chambers as instruments to alter consciousness. The below-world is where thresholds thin: where visions come, ancestors speak, and the living risk a controlled death to return changed.

Third, the subterranean as theatre of power. Nothing confers authority like mastery of a hidden path. Elites have carved restricted corridors beneath shrines and halls for processions, burials, water rites, or initiations. Control the door, control the narrative; control the narrative, control the people.

Fourth, the subterranean as a map of the cosmos. Across cultures, the world is tiered—upper, middle, lower—and movement between levels is the privilege of heroes, shamans, and sovereigns. The underworld harbors both terror and treasure: serpents coiled around roots of a world-tree, rivers that remember, judges who weigh hearts, and mothers who birth sunlight. To step below is to rehearse death and, sometimes, to steal fire.

Underworld Motifs Across World Mythologies
(Global Overview)

⌒ Serpent Gate   Π Twin Pillars   ◎ Labyrinth   ≋ Rivers of Dead
Schematic regional clusters (not precise sites)

The Pattern That Won't Die
- *Entrances marked by serpents, birds, or twin pillars*
- *Labyrinth or spiral motifs guiding descent*
- *A river/void to cross, often with a guardian*
- *A gift or technology "brought back" to the surface (grain, metallurgy, law, calendar)*
- *Return with taboo: the explorer is altered, obligated, or exiled*

The Psychological and Historical Roots of Subterranean Legends

The Descent as Archetype

Every culture scripts a descent narrative: a katabasis. It might be a god braving shadow to rescue a beloved, a hero bargaining with death, or a seeker apprenticing to the night. The shared grammar is striking: departure from the bright world; disorientation; encounter; ordeal; negotiation; return with a boon. These are not just stories about caves—they are stories about minds. The descent mirrors the inward turn: a movement past the surface chatter into the archaic, the pre-verbal, the body's museum of memory. The cave is the skull of the world; the skull is the cave of the self.

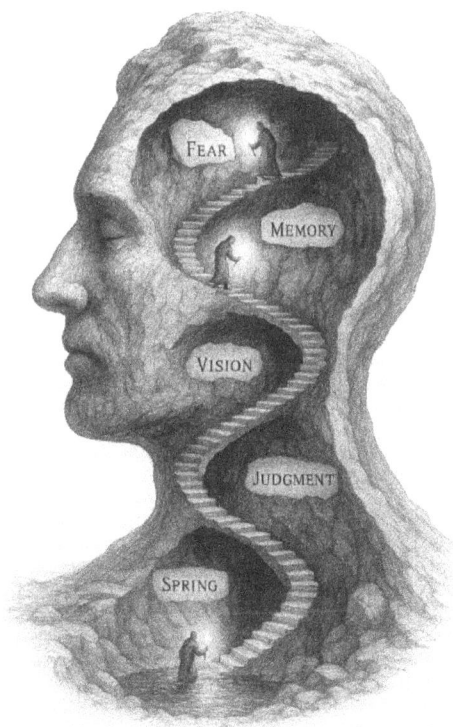

Ritual Architecture and the Engineered Below

Archaeology has repeatedly encountered engineered underground spaces at sacred centers: galleries, drains, hidden passages, womb-like chambers, and acoustic nodes designed to amplify chant or drum. This is architecture as technology for changing states and as stagecraft for revelation. Water—source, sound, mirror—is the favourite co-conspirator. Light is rationed. Airflow is planned. Access is controlled. The pilgrim confronts darkness, follows sound, and emerges into a small stone womb where the ritual climax unfolds.

Memory After Cataclysm

Subterranean legends also function as trauma archives. After floods, fires, or sky-borne disasters, survivors do what humans always do: encode warnings in a story. "Go below when the serpents return," one tale might say—serpents being a memory of comets or rivers of flame. "Follow the swallows to the deep halls," another might teach—swallows being the birds who find safe crevices. Over centuries, mnemonic becomes mythic, becomes sacred.

How Mainstream History Dismisses the Stories That Refuse to Die

Reading a Subterranean Myth like a Historian
- *Identify the practical layer (shelter, water, and defense).*
- *Identify the ritual layer (sound, light, procession, initiation).*
- *Identify the cosmological layer (tiers of the world, guardians, and trials).*
- *Identify the memory layer (encoded disaster, taboo, survival strategy).*
- *Ask how later elites reframed earlier practices to consolidate power.*

Let's name the elephant under the floorboards: a **knowledge filter** operates in every discipline. It isn't necessarily a conspiracy; it's a set of defaults. Evidence that fits prevailing models passes smoothly. Evidence that muddies the timeline, suggests contacts deemed impossible, or implies capabilities thought anachronistic gets stalled in quarantine: "outlier," "local oddity," "ritual," "hoax," "misdated," or simply "unpublished." Add practical limits—restricted sites, incomplete excavations, vanished field notes—and you have a structured silence.

Why do some subterranean stories chafe institutions so badly?

- **Timelines:** Chambers or tunnels that imply planning horizons unfashionable for the period.

- **Technology:** Precision feats underground (ventilation, acoustics, water management) that seem to leapfrog known toolkits.

- **Continuity:** Mythic motifs echoing across continents in ways that rekindle debates about diffusion vs. independent invention.

- **Access:** Temples, caves, and tunnels sealed "for safety" or "conservation," with glimpses filtered through small teams and tight reports.

None of this proves that every legend is literal. It does justify re-opening certain questions with better tools and a braver methodology.

…Message for You, the Explorer

Your role here is not as a spectator but a participant. Imagine this introduction as the threshold chamber. You've left the sunlit prologue; the air is cooler; the sound of your steps has changed. Take a breath. What follows is not a crusade to prove every claim true. It's a commitment to do the one thing most mythic traditions demand from a seeker: **follow the pattern with courage.**

When we meet a legend of a golden city under a mountain, we won't rush to build it in our heads. We'll ask: Where did the story start? What was happening locally—climate, conflict, trade? What geology sits underfoot? Who controlled access to the site? Which details remain stable across generations? Do new technologies (LIDAR, GPR, muon imaging, high-resolution satellite archaeology) illuminate anything the old debate missed? Where does the story function as a manual for survival, as a map of consciousness, and as a badge of identity?

We will keep both lamps lit: the lamp of wonder and the lamp of method.

The Knowledge Filter, in Plain Language
1. *Model first, data second. We often ask the past to confirm our expectations.*
2. *Career risk. Young researchers avoid results that ignite old controversies.*
3. *Site control. Gatekeepers—public and private—shape what can be studied and shown.*
4. *Language games. Labels can end a debate before it begins ("ritual object," "folk belief").*
5. *Public appetite. Dramatic finds are marketed; awkward ones are minimized.*

The Journey Ahead

The path through these buried realms is structured like a descent with waystations. Each part builds on the last, alternating between myth and measurable ground.

Part I — Hollow Worlds and Hidden Kingdoms.

We begin with the grand claims: the cosmic hollows, inner kingdoms of sages, and shining cities beneath deserts and ice. Rather than mock or worship these tales, we parse their core grammar and search for their roots in ritual geographies, climatic refugia, and political theatre.

Part II — Stone Under Skin: Real Subterranean Cities and Complexes.

Here we move from legend to rock. We examine multilevel underground cities, ceremonial labyrinths, engineered waterworks, and cave networks that served as habitations, sanctuaries, and theatres of initiation. The question isn't "did humans build underground?"— that's obvious—it's **how far** and **to what ends.**

Part III — Zones of Silence: Suppressed Lore and Sealed Doors.

This is where we evaluate claims of serpent guardians, forbidden corridors, redacted maps, and "no-go" caves. We will separate romance from record, but we won't ignore consistent testimony simply because it troubles tidy narratives.

Part IV — The Archetype Underground: Myth, Mind, and Science.

How to Travel This Book
- *Keep a double ledger: legend on the left, measurements on the right.*
- *Mark recurrences: when symbols and solutions repeat across distances.*
- *Note absences: what we are not shown, not told, not allowed to see.*
- *Ask why now: when a door is opened (or closed) in our time, who benefits?*
- *Stay accountable: wonder is not a license to abandon rigor.*

Finally, we return to the descent as an inner technology. We correlate visionary motifs from ritual caves and enclosed chambers with neuropsychology, acoustics, and controlled darkness—always asking: what does the mind do in stone-crafted night, and what did that mean for the birth of culture?

Workbook Bonus — Your Field Kit.

Maps, reading of topographies, questions to take into a site, and exercises for tracking the four layers of any subterranean story (practical, ritual, cosmological, and memory).

Raising the Stakes

It's tempting to treat underground legends as quaint. That would be a mistake. What lies below has always been civilization's insurance policy and its memory vault. In eras of climatic instability and geopolitical fracture—like ours—the prospect of engineered subterranean refuges moves from folklore to foresight. Meanwhile, a suite of technologies is making the ground more transparent than at any time in history:

- **Airborne LIDAR** peels forest canopies away to reveal gridded cities and causeways long erased at the surface.

- **Ground-Penetrating Radar (GPR)** detects voids, void-clusters, and buried walls beneath plazas and fields.

- **Muon radiography** reads density like an X-ray, charting chambers in massive structures.

- **Hyperspectral satellites** flag soil moisture anomalies—often the fingerprints of buried works.

- **Computational acoustics** reconstructs how enclosed spaces shape sound and, by extension, experience.

These tools won't make every legend literal—but they will salvage the salvageable. They help us update old maps with new contour lines and test recurring claims with non-destructive rigor. In other words, we are, perhaps for the first time, **technologically equipped to take myth seriously.**

A Credible Awe

This book will not require you to choose between enchantment and evidence. It requires you to **practice both.** When a legend of a luminous city in the desert refuses to die, your task is not to bow nor to sneer, but to ask patient, layered questions and to keep asking them even when the answers complicate careers and tidy categories. When excavations yield a passage no one expected, resist the reflex to call it "ritual" and move on; rituals are the densest code we have—decipher them.

We'll also honour the human reasons for secrecy. Not every closed door hides a scandal; some hide a prayer. Living communities have the right to protect sites that still breathe for them. Respect is not the enemy of curiosity; it is its spine.

Five Questions Our Century Can Finally Ask Underground
1. *What is the true extent of underground habitation in key regions (not just famous sites but their hinterlands)?*
2. *Which acoustic signatures suggest intentional design for trance or speech?*
3. *How do water systems (cisterns, channels, sumps) reveal ritual calendars and climate strategies?*
4. *Can we model processional routes from surface to chamber to understand initiation narratives?*
5. *Where do sealed spaces align with living traditions that still speak of taboos or guardians—and why?*

An Invitation—and a Challenge

Perhaps you have felt it: the quiet tug toward a cave mouth, a narrow stair in an old city, a cracked slab in a field, a breath of cold air rising where none should be. Perhaps you have dreamed of corridors and woke with the taste of damp stone on your tongue. These are not mere moods. They are the psyche's way of telling you something essential has been left **below.**

The chapters ahead will not flatter you with certainty, and they will not insult you with naïveté. They will ask you to hold tension: between mythic splendour and measurable rock, between the shimmering of visionary states and the grit of engineering, between what we want to be true and what the earth says when scanned, cored, and listened to. You will see that myths of buried realms persist because they are solutions—simultaneously to survival, sovereignty, spirituality, and science. You will also see that our moment in history is uniquely suited to test them.

We stand at a hinge in human self-knowledge. In the skies, instruments read starlight for planets we cannot visit. On the ground, instruments

---

The Ethics of Descent
- *Do no harm to living communities, sites, or ecosystems.*
- *Name uncertainty; distinguish between what is measured, inferred, and imagined.*
- *Share credit with local knowledge keepers.*
- *Refuse sensationalism that turns people's shrines into spectacle.*
- *Protect coordinates when disclosure invites looting or desecration.*

now read the earth for cities we have not yet admitted. Both endeavours widen us. Both ask for humility.

The buried realms are waiting. The question is—will we finally dare to enter?

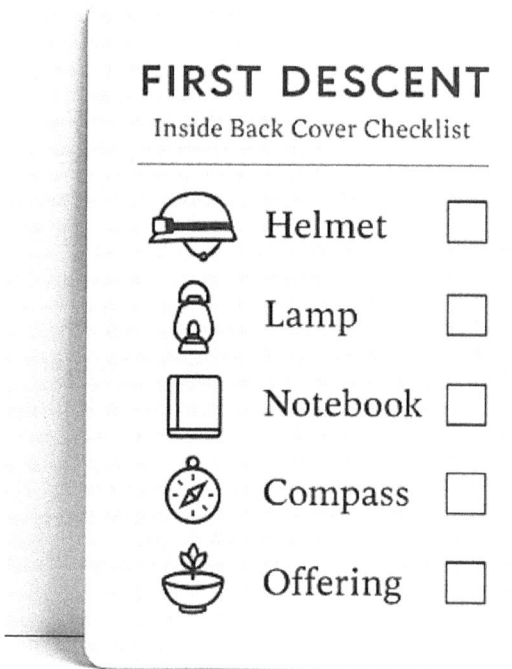

FIRST DESCENT
Inside Back Cover Checklist

🪖 Helmet ☐

🏮 Lamp ☐

📓 Notebook ☐

🧭 Compass ☐

🌱 Offering ☐

A Glimpse of What Comes Next

- **From Hollow Earth to Hollow Mountain:** Why 'world-inside-world' narratives bloom at cultural frontiers, and what their stable symbols predict about real topographies.

- **Cities Under Stone:** A guided tour of true subterranean habitations and ritual networks—how they were carved, ventilated, defended, and experienced.

- **Serpents, Seals, and Silent Zones:** Sorting measured walls from rumour, and taboo from power play.

- **The Inner Descent:** How engineered darkness, controlled acoustics, fasting, and plant sacraments created repeatable states that seeded art, calendar, and kingship.

Closing Affirmation

You are not asked to believe. You are asked to **notice** and to **follow**. The discipline we'll practice is curiosity with a backbone.

Now: take your lamp. Put your palm to the cool wall. Feel the old air rise. Step through.

The descent begins.

---

iField Notes: Your First Descent
- *Before: Learn the geology. Pack respect. Ask permission. Bring two lights. Tell someone your plan.*
- *During: Listen to sound; note shifts in temperature and airflow; sketch routes; record feelings as data.*
- *After: Journal immediately. Map myth motifs to observations. Share responsibly.*

Part I: Legends of the Hollow Earth

Chapter 1: The Hollow Earth Hypothesis

The wind knifes across a white world without edges. Ahead, a bruised halo hangs low over the horizon—heat mirage or the blurred rim of something vaster? Imagine stepping toward that haze knowing legends insist it's not just weather, but a rim to another realm: a mouth in the planet, a passage down. This is where our journey begins—not with answers, but with a feeling: that beneath the mapped crust of Earth, a second cartography waits, spooling through caves, myths, polar mists, and the recesses of our oldest stories.

You and I are going to interrogate that feeling—carefully, curiously, and with both boots on the ground.

From Ancient Cosmologies to Modern Conspiracies

Long before anyone spoke of "Hollow Earth," human cultures imagined layered worlds: upper, middle, and under. Shamans the world over depicted caves and clefts as portals—thresholds where human perception thins and "below" becomes a theatre for encounters with teachers, beasts, and the dead. Rock shelters and deep caverns, daubed with beings that are part-animal, part-human, read like maps of a cosmos with trapdoors. These are not engineering diagrams of a geophysical hole; they are psychogeography's ritual topologies for crossing between states.

What the stories share:

- A vertical axis (rooted in caves, mountains, or tree-like pillars) linking realms.

- Gatekeepers or guides (vultures, serpents, twins, hooded figures).

- A claim that knowledge—medicine, metal, order—arrives from "elsewhere" via subterranean or underworld channels.

In the Near East, Neolithic sanctuaries show an obsession with thresholds, rebirth, and the transit of souls—motifs later reframed as "underworld journeys." Iconography of birds of prey and apertures (or "soul holes") implies passages for the deceased and for initiates who simulate death to learn the sky-codes of life. This archaeology animates the oldest strata of the hollow-world idea: not a cavern you could fly into, but an initiatory descent enabling transformation.

Modern conspiracy culture reframes these symbolic geographies into literal engineering: a physically hollow Earth with polar entrances, hidden suns, and advanced civilizations. The move from myth to mechanism is seductive because it promises proof. But it risks flattening—and misunderstanding—what the oldest evidence likely intended to convey.

Understand the Shift

Mythic Underworld → Mechanical Hollow
- *Mythic underworld: ritual, psyche, death-rebirth, encoded astronomy.*
- *Mechanical hollow: ice-rimmed tunnels, inner suns, fleets and bases.*

Takeaway: Don't mistake a ritual map for a flight plan.

The Hollow Earth Hypothesis: A Short History of a Big Idea

Early modern seeds. In the 17th–18th centuries, natural philosophers wrestling with magnetism, auroras, and earthquakes proposed layered or hollow interiors—nested shells or cavernous strata—to reconcile phenomena they couldn't yet measure. These were thought experiments stitched to the edge of available data.

Romantic and pulp expansions. The 19th–20th centuries fused polar exploration with romance and pseudo-ethnography. The motif ripened into a full narrative: openings at the poles; temperate lands under the ice; hidden suns; "older races." This is where *The Smoky God* and Symmes' "holes" enter the scene.

Archaeological counterpoint. Meanwhile, the real underworlds we can excavate—catacombs, subterranean cities (think of Anatolian multilevel complexes), and ritual pits—tell a different story: people consistently built down for refuge, memory, and rite. They are human solutions to chaos, not proofs of a planetary void.

> ### *Real Vs. Fantastic Subterrains*
> - *Real: lava tubes, limestone karst systems, hand-hewn cities, burial catacombs.*
> - *Fantastic: global cavity with polar inlets, central sun, lost super-civilizations.*
>
> *Key question to hold: What do the genuine subterranean worlds tell us about why "below" fascinates us?*

Symmes' Hole, The Smoky God, and the Myth of Polar Entrances

Symmes' Circular: The 1818 Spark

John Cleves Symmes Jr., a veteran with a flair for spectacle, circulated a bold claim: the planet is hollow, with vast interior spaces accessible through large openings at the poles. He petitioned Congress to fund an expedition. He never found his holes, but he left a conceptual crater in the popular imagination. The trope of "polar entrances" became a recurring archway for later tales, maps, and speculative diagrams.

Why it stuck:

- **Visibility gap.** Polar mists, temperature inversions, and mirages make horizons uncanny—perfect canvases for longing and misinterpretation.

- **Frontier fever.** The poles symbolized the last blank spaces on maps—ideal for hiding wonders.

- **Cultural hunger.** America loved self-authoring myths; Symmes fed that appetite.

The Smoky God (1908): The Novel That Read Like a Confession

Willis George Emerson's yarn recounts Norwegian sailor Olaf Jansen, who allegedly drifts through a polar portal into a temperate interior lit by a smoky central sun, meets benevolent giants, and returns to scorn. It's a classic of "I have seen what they deny" literature: personal testimony, grand scenery, gentle superiors, betrayal by authorities.

What the tale exploits well:

- **Compassionate interiors.** Inner lands aren't just secret; they're ethical upgrades to a cruel surface.

- **Reverse colonization.** The "inside" civilizes the "outside," flipping the usual script.

- **Smoky sun symbolism.** A twilight lamp for a world of second chances.

But as evidence, it tumbles: the physics of an interior sun fail; seismology contradicts cavernous interiors; and no independent log supports a claimed transit. The book is significant culturally, not geographically.

Case Study: Admiral Byrd's Alleged Secret Antarctic Diary

No figure is invoked more in Hollow Earth lore than Admiral Richard E. Byrd. The *claim*: a secret diary reveals he flew through an Antarctic opening into a lush inner land populated by advanced beings who warned humanity about nuclear folly. The *context*: Byrd was a real polar pioneer (1920s–1950s), and his expeditions—especially Operation High Jump (1946–47)—were vast and, in part, military.

Why the story persists:

- **Perfect witness.** Byrd had credibility, aviation reach, and access to the last wilderness.

- **Cold War anxiety.** The idea that "unknown powers" issued moral warnings resonated.

- **Document mystique.** "Suppressed diaries" are the grail of alternative history.

What the record and physics suggest:

- **Flight profiles.** Known flight ranges, fuel constraints, and weather windows make a deep interior transit implausible.

- **Seismology & geodesy.** Earth's interior structure—mapped by seismic waves—shows solid and liquid layers, not a habitable cavity.

- **Source chain.** The "diary" surfaces in fringe publications decades later, with no verifiable provenance; internal stylistic quirks don't match Byrd's documented writing.

Balanced verdict: Byrd's *authentic* achievements stand. The "secret diary" remains a story about desire—for guardians, for hidden warnings, for being chosen—rather than a credible flight record.

Byrd, Facts We Can Stand On

- *Historic polar flights and bases are well-documented.*
- *Operation High Jump's logistics (ships, aircraft, and weather losses) are a matter of record.*
- *No contemporaneous official documents corroborate an interior landfall.*

Archaeology, Myth, and the Descent Motif

The most valuable way to read Hollow Earth is as a modern echo of a far older human grammar: descent for knowledge, return with gifts. Deep time cultures encode this grammar in stone, art, and ceremony:

- **Cave as portal.** Many traditions depict caves as thresholds where initiates meet "teachers"—figures that challenge, heal, or impart skills. Across continents, this underworld encounter is part of becoming fully human.

- **Bird psychopomps.** Vultures and raptors—often carved or incised—guide souls between realms; apertures in stone (sometimes literally "holes" in monuments) stage the passage. This is not a geological hollow; it's a ritual technology of transition.

- **Cataclysm memory.** Flood and fire myths suggest ancestral recollections of upheaval. Later authors spin these into grand migrations and lost homelands—a narrative compost that modern hollow-world stories draw from, even when evidence points elsewhere.

Why it matters: Mythic descents aren't mistakes about geology; they're accurate maps of human experience at thresholds—illness, initiation, bereavement, altered states—refracted through sacred places.

> ### Three Keys To Descent Narratives
> 1. *The Gate: a marked opening (cave, chamber, stone ring) that tells you: the ordinary rules pause here.*
> 2. *The Guide: a bird, serpent, twin, or hooded figure who "knows the way."*
> 3. *The Gift: a skill, law, song, or agriculture—what returns with you to repair the tribe.*

Gate, Guide, Gift — Neolithic Portal Stone & Vulture Motif (Anatolia–Levant)

Science Weighs In: What Earth Is (and Isn't)

The most rigorous tests of a hollow planet come from physics and Earth science:

- **Seismic tomography.** Earthquakes send P-waves and S-waves through the planet. Their travel times, reflections, and shadows map an inner structure: solid inner core, liquid outer core, viscous mantle, brittle crust. No signal behaves as if crossing a vast air-filled cavity.

- **Gravity & moment of inertia.** Earth's mass and spin properties match a dense interior; a hollow would shift these numbers dramatically.

- **Magnetic field.** The geodynamo—electrically conducting fluid in the outer core—requires the very interior Hollow Earth rejects.

- **Heat flow.** Observed geothermal gradients and plate tectonics derive from a convecting mantle and hot core, not a sunlit internal Eden.

Polar illusions: Temperature inversions and Fata Morgana mirages distort horizons—sometimes stacking and bending landscapes into "cliffs," "leads," or "openings." In the age of Symmes and after, such optics helped hang a mask on the ice.

What good science doesn't kill: Wonder. It just moves it—away from fantasies of a shell-world toward amazement that a molten heart and shifting plates created the niche we inhabit.

Why We Keep Looking Down: Psychology of the Hollow

Three needs power the Hollow Earth's persistence:

1. **The need for guardians.** In chaotic centuries, it comforts to imagine wiser beings tucked just below the floorboards, ready to intervene.

2. **The need for hope.** A green interior is the fantasy of a second chance: Eden restored, accessible without dying—just descending.

3. **The need for agency.** If "they" hide it, then "we" can uncover it. The discovery fantasy returns control to the seeker.

When read this way, Symmes, *The Smoky God*, and the Byrd "diary" aren't errors; they're temperature checks on our civilizational mood. They show spikes of fear and hunger—and an ache to belong to a cosmos with guides.

PSYCHOLOGICAL ICEBERG

Visible tip: *Claims* · Hidden layers: *Mistrust · Hope · Belonging · Initiation*

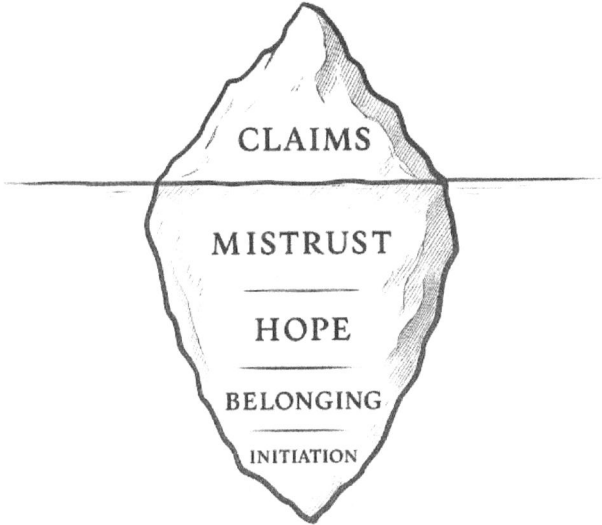

CLAIMS

MISTRUST

HOPE

BELONGING

INITIATION

A Field Guide To Subterranean Longing
- *Symptom: "They won't tell us."*
- *Root cause: Mistrust harvested from real secrecy elsewhere.*
- *Antidote: Build shared, checkable evidence—then let myth do what it does best: nourish meaning, not masquerade as measurement.*

Threads from Deep Time: Caves, Vultures, and Star Roads

A final synthesis brings archaeology and myth into sharper relief:

- **Stone sanctuaries and "soul holes."** Circular apertures in prehistoric enclosures function as ritual portals, linking the human dead with cyclical skies. They appear beside avian motifs that cue a psychopompic role: the bird carries prayers where humans cannot.

- **Cave visions and teachers.** Cross-cultural accounts of initiatory voyages—whether induced by sensory deprivation, drumming, plant sacraments, or prolonged darkness—feature encounters in "other-below" spaces with entities framed as healers or instructors. This underworld isn't a cavern you can charter a plane into; it's a reliable, structured landscape of mind and ceremony.

- **Cataclysm memory and refuges.** Flood, fire, and winter myths preserve a memory of survival through descent into caves, into mountains, into engineered shelter. Later romanticizers welded these into continental sagas, proposing sunken motherlands and dispersed colonies—schemes that, though compelling, outrun the sober reading of evidence.

A fair reading of "Buried Realms" therefore yields two truths at once:

1. The human underworld is real—ritual, psychological, archaeological—and it has taught us for millennia.

2. The mechanical Hollow Earth is, so far, a story—fruitful as metaphor, thin as measurement.

Reading the Fringe Without Losing the Plot

You're going to encounter more claims: secret bases, inner suns, maps of tunnels under every mountain range. Here's how to stay open and rigorous:

- **Verify provenance.** Who held the document when, and can that chain be independently checked?

- **Separate genre from geology.** A compelling *narrative* is not inherently *evidence.*

- **Cross with hard data.** Seismic profiles, gravity, and heat flow—if a claim contradicts multiple independent datasets, it requires extraordinary new evidence.

- **Salvage the symbol.** Even when the mechanism falls, the myth may point to real human needs: initiation, refuge, repair.

This book's title promises **buried realms** and **refusals**—and we've honoured both. There *are* realms buried in stone and mind. There *are* refusals—sometimes by institutions that hoard information poorly, and sometimes by us, when we refuse the patient discipline of inquiry in favour of certainty's sugar high.

In the chapters ahead, we'll keep that balance: chase the marvel, test it hard, and, when the mechanism collapses, ask what the myth was trying to feed all along.

Working Principles for Our Expedition

1. **Atmospheric yet credible:** We'll keep the wonder and keep the data.

2. **Inclusive:** You're not an audience; you're on the rope beside me.

3. **Balanced:** Myth *and* measurement, side by side.

4. **Curiosity-driven:** Each answer must sharpen, not dull, the next question.

camera   trowel   magnetometer   notebook

How Archaeology Meets Myth

Pattern: portals, avian guides, rebirth symbolism.

- **Practice:** curated descent—fasting, darkness, drumming, plant sacraments—to enter the "underworld," learn, return.

- **Places:** stone enclosures with apertures and avian iconography (threshold architectures).

Timeline: Hollow Earth, At a Glance
- *Ancient & prehistoric: descent rites, cave art, bird psychopomps, ritual apertures (underworld as initiation).*
- *17th–18th c.: speculative inner shells to explain magnetism & quakes (proto-science).*
- *1818: Symmes' circular ignites public fascination with polar openings.*
- *Late 19th–early 20th c.: pulp and "found narrative" era, e.g., The Smoky God.*
- *Mid-20th c.: Byrd's real feats and a fake "secret diary" fuse into Cold-War myth.*
- *Late 20th–21st c.: Internet era formalizes lore; scientific evidence against mechanical hollowness becomes comprehensive.*

Cautionary Note On "Suppressed Evidence

Some critiques of academic gatekeeping point to genuine blind spots and biases. That history exists—and it's worth studying. But "suppressed" is not a magic word that turns fiction into fact. Demand rigor from *both* orthodoxy and dissent. (For a meta-history of how unusual claims and anomalies have been argued over—sometimes fairly, sometimes not—see discussions that catalog the sociology of evidence in human-origin debates.)

Notes on Sources and Lens

- **Shamanic underworlds & cave visions:** Cross-cultural accounts of initiatory descent and "teachers" in altered states inform the lens used here to read "below" as a ritual topography.

- **Neolithic thresholds, birds, and "soul holes":** Archaeological motifs of avian psychopomps and apertures at cult sites inspire the portal reading used throughout.

- **Cataclysm memory & lost homelands:** Classic comparative attempts to link flood traditions and civilizational parallels shaped later subterranean mythmaking—even where the literal models do not stand.

- **Anomalies & academic argument:** The sociology of how evidence is accepted or sidelined is relevant—and a caution both ways.

The Descent We Can Make

If there's a doorway we can stand before today, it's not at the pole; it's in how we read. Before the next tale of ice-rimmed inlets and inner suns, pause at the lintel. Ask: Is this a ritual map posing as a flight plan? Is this a medicine story wearing a uniform? Is it a warning, consolation, or a dare?

Then step through—with your eyes open.

Chapter 2

Shambhala and Agartha

Close your eyes and imagine a map of the world where the most important borders aren't the ones we can see. No dotted lines, no colour blocks—only thresholds: cave mouths that breathe, hidden valleys that never thaw, flickers of gold at the edges of a glacier where no gold should be. When we trace this other atlas—drawn in chants, mantras, folktales, and the vague directions of travellers who swore they didn't dream—we keep running into two names: **Shambhala** and **Agartha**.

They are not "places" in the way an airport is a place. They behave more like **conditions**—states of access that must be earned. Buddhist adepts say Shambhala is a **pure realm** concealed in plain sight, veiled from those who have not purified perception. Esotericists whisper that Agartha is a **subterranean federation**—an ancient network of cities and sanctuaries beneath mountains and deserts, its scholars and sages quietly stewarding the surface world through cycles of rise and fall.

If this sounds romantic, it is. But romance isn't the opposite of truth. In this chapter, we'll move like field scientists through legend: reading the scriptures, tracking clues through Himalayan passes and desert sinkholes, testing claims against geology, archaeology, and cognition. We will be faithful to wonder **and** rigorous with evidence.

Shambhala in the Buddhist Imagination

Shambhala enters world literature through the **Kalachakra** ("Wheel of Time") tradition of Tibetan Buddhism. In these texts, Shambhala is presented as both **topography** and **topology**—a hidden kingdom with a capital (often named **Kalapa**) and an enlightened polity led by a lineage of **Kalki** or **Dharmaraja** kings, but also a diagram of the mind: a mandala you inhabit rather than merely visualize.

Descriptions vary, but certain features recur:

- A high-altitude realm encircled by a ring of snow mountains and protective winds—visible to those with karmic alignment, undecipherable to the merely curious.

- An ethical economy: abundance without excess, technology guided by compassion, governance as a **yogic art.**

- A prophecy: in an age of spiritual decline, Shambhala will reveal itself; the final Kalki—sometimes called **Rudra Chakrin**—leads a great turning that restores balance.

Two key interpretive currents developed over time:

1. **Exoteric-Symbolic Reading:** Shambhala is primarily internal. Its geography sketches a **roadmap of meditation**—outer mountains as inner obstacles, the capital as the **heart center** where wisdom and method unify. On this reading, the prophesied "battle" is the practitioner's victory over aggression, ignorance, and fear.

2. **Esoteric-Geographical Reading:** Shambhala is also, or even mainly, a **hidden polity** somewhere in inner Asia—reachable by rare passes or by the right ritual sequence at the right place. The realm is **subtle but tangible**, encoded in toponyms and guarded by vows.

In practice, advanced teachers have often held both views at once: Shambhala is **real** as mind—and **real** as place to those whose minds make that level of reality accessible.

Hindu Gateways to the Underworld

Where Buddhism speaks of Shambhala, Hindu cosmology offers a stacked universe of **lokas** (worlds), including subterranean realms like

Pātāla and **Nāga-loka**. These are not mere hells. They are **brilliant under-realms**—palaced, jewelled, ruled by nāga serpents and asura clans, irrigated by underground rivers, lit by **phosphorescent trees** and gems. In many Puranic passages, the underworld is morally **ambiguous**: it harbors both threat and wisdom.

Key motifs:

- **Nāgas** as guardians of knowledge, fertility, and hidden treasure.

- **Siddhas** and **yogins** dwelling in **guhā** (caves) as literal retreats and metaphors for the heart-cave.

- **Tunnels** beneath pilgrimage sites (tirthas) suggest ritual thresholds between strata of being.

While Pātāla is sometimes framed as a domain below the earth, the Sanskrit root *pat-* ("to fall") and the frequent pairing of caves with **inner realization** cues a dual reading: **underworld** equals **under-ego**— layers below the hurried daylight of ordinary mind.

Agartha: The Esoteric Federation Below

What to Remember about Shambhala?
- *Not a fantasy utopia, but a training model for enlightened society.*
- *Reveals the ethics of secrecy: concealment not to hoard power, but to protect the unready from their own projections.*
- *Prophecy frames responsibility: the "end times" are a call to practice, not an excuse to wait for rescue.*

"Agartha" (often spelled Agart(h)a, Agharta, or Agarttha) appears later than Shambhala in the historical record and gathers strands from India, the Himalayas, Central Asia, and Western occultism. In the most **coherent esoteric synthesis**, Agartha is a **network** rather than a single city—**a confederation of subterranean sanctuaries** linked by tunnels, lava tubes, and "soft spots" in the crust where limestone karst, basalt flows, or ancient riverbeds make large cavities possible.

Core propositions attributed to the Agartha tradition:

- Antiquity: The network predates recorded history, expanding cyclically as surface cultures collapse and contract.

- Stewardship: Adept in these cities, steward of repositories of **text, art, seed, and science**, surfacing in times of need with just enough influence to avert catastrophes or seed renaissances.

- Access Protocols: Entry is not a matter of maps, but of **moral resonance**—a test of humility, discipline, and service. Those who force entry cannot remain.

The picture is compelling because it **rationalizes a huge family of motifs**—from "people under the mountain" tales to long-distance sacred alignments—without requiring science-fiction geology. Think **many small realms**, not one hollow Earth.

Cross-Cultural Echoes: Grotto-Heavens and Underworld Courts

To keep ourselves honest, we compare. Around the world, elite or sacred knowledge is often **stored 'under'**:

- **Daoist Grotto-Heavens (洞天, *dongtian*):** mountain sanctuaries entered through thresholds that are both physical and visionary; each cave-heaven corresponds to a cosmogram and a regimen of internal alchemy.

- **Mesoamerican Xibalba:** a daunting underworld of trials that initiates must pass—part geography, part **psychodrama**.

- **Greek katabasis** (Orpheus, Odysseus): descents to retrieve wisdom or loved ones; caves as **curriculum**.

- **Celtic sídhe mounds:** time-dilated halls under hills where ethics, artistry, and power are tested.

These parallels don't prove Agartha exists; they **prove** humans everywhere instinctively **situate initiation below light level**—because the **brain** and **society** both change under conditions of silence, fluorescence, pressure, and isolation.

| Daoist grotto | Maya cave | Greek hero descend | Irish passage tomb |

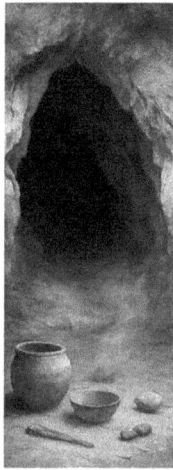

Ground-Truthing the Myths: Geology and Feasibility

Let's put on hard hats.

What the Earth Looks Like (Macro-Scale):

- Crust thickness: ~5–70 km (thin under oceans, thick under continents).

- Mantle: hot, plastic rock; **no giant habitable cavities.**

- Core: iron alloy; off the table for strolling sages.

- Seismology gives us exquisite constraints: **there is no global empty shell.**

What Nature Does Offer (Meso- and Micro-Scale):

- **Karst systems** (limestone + water): huge cave networks (hundreds of kilometres), stable chambers, subterranean rivers.

- **Lava tubes** (basaltic flows): long, smooth tunnels (tens of kilometres) with skylights and branches—common under volcanic fields and shield volcanoes.

- **Tectonic voids & talus caverns:** smaller, less stable, but numerous in mountains.

- **Salt caves:** sprawling but changeable.

- **Glacial and subglacial caverns:** transient; not suited to long-term habitation.

A **distributed Agartha** could hide in the interstices nature does allow: karst belts, basalt fields, and mountain roots riddled with fractures—especially if its "cities" are **modest in scale** and **camouflaged** behind ordinary cave systems.

Environmental Constraints:

- **Air:** Ventilation is the limiting factor. Yet multi-entranced karst plus engineered shafts can move air effectively.

- **Water**: Subterranean rivers are abundant in karst; water is soluble.

- **Light**: Torches → oils → bioluminescence → electricity. Historically, communities can thrive with very little light via circadian discipline.

- **Food**: The bottleneck. Mushroom, algae, insect, and aquaculture can supplement, but a large subterranean population needs **surface trade** or high-yield hydroponics powered by underground streams or geothermal gradients.

Conclusion: A **continuous hollow Earth** is impossible. A **patchwork of habitable nodes** connected by natural and engineered passages is **plausible**—especially if the true "population" is small, secretive, and intermittently supplied from the surface.

KARST AQUIFER & BASALT LAVA TUBES

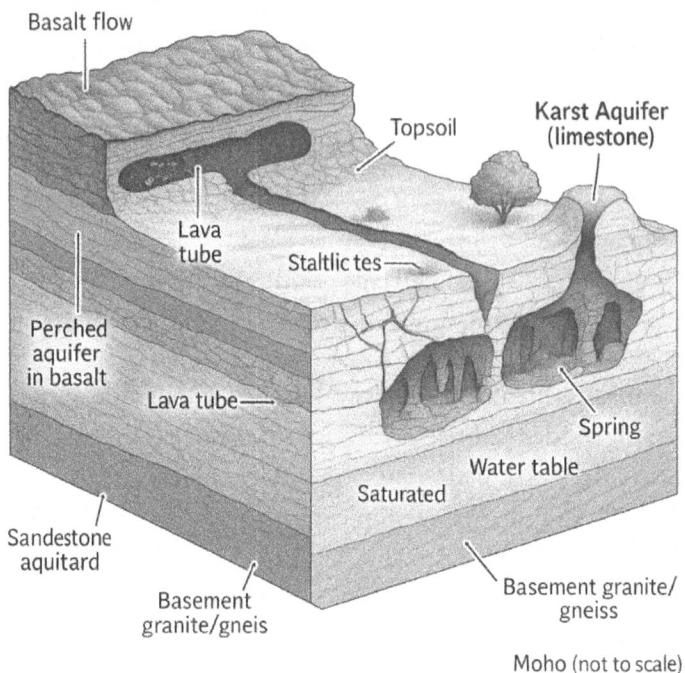

Basalt flow

Topsoil

Karst Aquifer
(limestone)

Lava
tube

Staltlic tes

Perched
aquifer
in basalt

Lava tube

Spring

Water table

Saturated

Sandestone
aquitard

Basement
granite/gneis

Basement granite/
gneiss

Moho (not to scale)

Archaeology of the Underneath: What We Can Visit

The temptation is to equate **every** underground complex with Agartha.
We must resist that. But we can log **precedents**—proofs of human
capacity for deep, expansive subterranean life:

- **Cappadocia's rock-cut cities:** Multilevel underground towns
  carved into tuff—airshafts, stables, kitchens, churches—
  capable of sheltering thousands in times of danger.

- **Hypogeum sanctuaries:** Catacombs and ritual complexes with
  acoustic design that induces **trance-ready resonance.**

- **Monastic cave systems:** From India's Ajanta and Ellora to Chinese cliff grottoes and Himalayan meditation caves—evidence of **long-term subterranean habitation by choice.**

- **Wartime and refuge networks:** Medieval to modern complexes with storage, command rooms, and even hospitals.

These do not "prove Agartha," but they **normalize** the idea that human beings carve, expand, and **culture** the underworld at scale—sometimes with astonishing engineering.

Esoteric Accounts of a Subterranean Paradise

Across travellers' notebooks and initiatory lineages, a consistent set of **signals** appears when people claim contact with hidden cities:

- **Qualities of Light:** reports of "skyless daylight"—caverns lit by crystals, cold light, or diffuse glow. (Physics allows **bioluminescence** and **engineered lighting**; esoterically, light is often a **metaphor for mind.**)

- **Temporal Slippage:** time felt **longer** or **shorter**; returnees swear they were gone for hours when days passed, or the reverse. (Known **cognitive phenomena** under sensory isolation; also a ritual dramatization of threshold crossing.)

- **Tone of Civility:** inhabitants described as **courteous, precise, and inwardly strong**; conversation feels like **instruction** more than socializing.

- **Selective Revelation:** visitors are allowed to see **only what is necessary**; exits are not in the same place as entrances; maps are **discouraged.**

What makes these accounts valuable is not whether they are "literally" true in the way we demand of GPS, but that they **agree on function:**

Agartha/ Shambhala appears to enact pedagogy. You don't go there to be impressed; you go there to be **changed**.

How the Mind Makes a Paradise
- *The qualities reported (silence, clean air, stable temperature, periodic light, ritual diet) optimize cognition.*
- *Cave acoustics + chant = reliable access to altered states.*
- *Carefully staged novelty (architecture, etiquette) breaks habitual thought.*
- *"Paradise" here is not luxury—it's a well-tuned school.*

Case Study: Theosophy and the 'Inner Earth Masters'

In the late nineteenth and early twentieth centuries, Western esoteric circles popularized a story of **Hidden Masters**—advanced adepts guiding humanity from seclusion. As the meme evolved, some strands explicitly located these teachers in **subterranean** or **remote Himalayan** retreats and linked them to a **Shambhala/Agartha axis.**

What to extract—and how to read it critically yet fairly:

- **Transmission Claim:** Adepts train pupils (chelas) over long arcs, sometimes by correspondence or seemingly impossible **mind-to-mind** contact. The lore insists **lineage matters** more than place.

- **Localization Drift:** Initially, "mountain retreats," later retellings locate these sanctuaries **underground** with more architectural specificity—an imaginative **deepening** consistent with the era's fascination with exploration, mining, and tunnels.

- **Ethical Curriculum:** The Master's chief concern is **motive:** they screen for humility, perseverance, and a willingness to serve rather than to merely know.

- **Points of Tension:** Challenges around authentication, forged communications, and charisma gone wrong. Any living tradition invites misuse; provenance must be **tested**, not taken on faith.

A disciplined way forward:

1. Treat the Masters tradition as an **applied ethics school** disguised as adventure.

2. Separate **pedagogy** (valuable) from **pageantry** (negotiable).

3. When "Inner Earth" claims appear, evaluate with the **geology/archaeology** filters we've built: small is plausible, planet-sized is not.

Cartographies of Access: How One Would Look

If we were planning a sober expedition, we wouldn't chase **romance**; we'd chase **constraints**:

- **Toponymy:** Map "snake," "dragon," "jewel," "hidden gate," and "wind door" place-names across karst belts and basaltic provinces in the Himalayas, Pamirs, Altai, and Anatolia.

- **Hydrology:** Overlay subterranean river systems; look for poljes, sinkholes, resurgences—places where **entry is natural**.

- **Acoustics & Ritual Archaeology:** Identify caves with evidence of **chant-friendly architecture**—niches, resonant domes, flat platforms—and nearby hermit cells.

- **Ethnography:** Build long-term trust with mountain communities; listen for **quiet stories**—not spectacular myths but **odd practical details** (a wind that sings on certain days; a ridge that "steams" in winter).

We would go less as treasure hunters and more as **librarians**, indexing patterns without forcing them into a single theory. If "Agartha" is emergent anywhere, it will **announce itself** in the **density of correlations**—pragmatic, low-key, cumulative.

The Psychology of 'Below': Why the Underworld Endures

Humans descend for three synergistic reasons:

1. **Biology:** Darkness and silence trigger **default-mode network** shifts, revealing patterns and insights inaccessible in sensory noise.

2. **Social Design:** Underground settings support **monastic economies**—small, stable, low-variance communities optimized for study and practice.

3. **Mythic Pressure:** Stories must **go somewhere**. Descent is the oldest dramaturgy: breakdown → initiation → return.

Shambhala–Agartha endures because it **harmonizes** with these necessities. The legends' staying power is not only a matter of belief; it's a matter of **fit**—between landscape, brain, and culture.

The Prophecy Question: Cycles, Crises, and Responsibility

Prophecies surrounding Shambhala often climax in a **turning**: at a nadir of ethics, the hidden realm intervenes. Read flatly, this tempts fatalism: **wait** for rescue. Read skilfully, it calls for **distributed leadership: be** the "Kalki" in your square kilometre.

> ***How to Build Your Own 'Gateway'***
> - *Practice ethical minimalism for 40 days (speech, diet, sleep).*
> - *Study breath-sound in resonant spaces (even a stairwell).*
> - *Treat silence as a teacher, not a void.*
> - *Ask not "Where is Shambhala?" but "When am I Shambhala-ready?"*

Consider a practical, non-apocalyptic reading:

- The "dark age" is a **distraction** at an industrial scale.

- The "war" is **attention vs. extraction.**

- The "weapon" is **abiding awareness** coupled with **techniques governed by compassion.**

On this interpretation, Shambhala reveals itself **whenever** communities practice **lucid governance** and **careful craft**—in monasteries, labs, farms, start-ups, and, yes, in certain caves.

Field Notes from Known Thresholds

Without romanticizing, we can learn from living places where "below" already disciplines life:

- **Himalayan hermitages**: micro-societies oriented around a cave, spring, and a code of conduct; small "Shambhalas" in everything but scale.

- **Desert lava fields**: lava tubes as seasonal refuges; air moves, water condenses, silence teaches.

- **Karst monasteries**: courtyards sunk into limestone; acoustics used to train attention; troglophilic gardens (mushrooms, shade herbs).

These are **Shambhala-adjacent**: not the fabled city, but its **grammar** in practice—ethics + engineering + attention.

Common Objections, Clear Answers

"Isn't a hollow Earth impossible?"

Correct—and also a straw man. The strongest **Shambhala/Agartha** readings never require a planetary balloon. They posit **many small, selective spaces**, which geology allows.

"Why no conclusive photos?"

Because if your model claims **selective permeability**, the lack of mass media proof is **predictive**, not evasive. High-traffic caves are not the ones with thresholds.

"Is this cultural appropriation?"

It can be—unless we **center source traditions**, respect **safeguards**, and **translate responsibly**. The point is not to cannibalize myth but to **let it tutor conduct**.

"Couldn't all of this be psychological?"

Yes—and. The psychological does not negate the physical; it **conditions access** to it. In every tradition, ethical and attentional training is the **gate technology**.

Working Hypothesis: Shambhala and Agartha as One Ecology

Rather than pit them against each other—Shambhala (pure realm) vs. Agartha (underground confederation)—treat them as **coextensive**:

- **Shambhala** is the **operating system**—a dharmic social design that optimizes the mind.

- **Agartha** is the **hardware layer**—actual carved, tuned, and hidden spaces where that OS can run at high fidelity.

Sometimes Shambhala is **only** a state of mind; sometimes it **also** has an address. Either way, the entrance requires **the same prerequisites**: ethics, practice, and service.

Chapter 3

Hell, Hades, and the Underworld

You feel it the moment you step into a cave: the temperature drops, sound turns to felted echoes, and the air smells like wet stone and older things. Every instinct says "watch your footing," but a subtler intuition whispers "listen." For as long as there have been people to wonder where the dead go, the entrances to that question—literal and figurative—have so often been holes in the earth: caverns, chasms, sinkholes, the black mouths of cenotes and mountain grottoes.

This chapter is our guided descent into those mouths—Greek Hades, Norse Hel, and Maya Xibalba—and the archetypal pattern of going down so that something in us may come up transformed. We'll travel as co-investigators, weighing legend against archaeology, myth against measurable residues of ritual—charcoal, calcite, bones; footprints and footpaths under stalactites; and in all cases the human insistence on portals: thresholds where the ordinary world thins and another world presses back.

Along the way, we will not simply retell underworld stories. We will read them as field notes on the most recurring journey in human culture: the descent (katabasis), the ordeal, the encounter, and the return with knowledge or power. We will also maintain an open case file on the practical applications of caves, including shrines, places for initiations, stages for altered states, and long, rock-lined corridors mapped onto the sky in unexpected ways. Ethnography and cognitive archaeology show why these spaces so reliably behave like "gates"—how darkness, silence, and isolation can push the brain into visionary modes that ancient communities learned to harness and interpret. In this, caves become the oldest classrooms on earth for the oldest subject on earth: what to do about death.

The Cave as a Device

Caves are not just places; they are technologies. Darkness and sensory deprivation induce altered states; winding passages emulate symbolic death and rebirth; acoustics magnify chant and heartbeat. Archaeology suggests many cultures intentionally used caves to stage initiations that mirrored a descent to the dead—and a return.

Ancient Greek, Norse, and Mayan Visions of the Underworld

A. Hades: The City of Shades and the Contract of Return

The Greek underworld is neither simple hellfire nor mere oblivion; it is a complex geography with rivers (Acheron, Styx, Lethe), ferries, gates, and districts for both the wicked and the heroic. Hermes Psychopomp leads the newly dead to the ferryman; coins sealed in the mouth pay the fare; oaths sworn on the Styx supposedly bind even gods. The Greek vision is not just a map of the afterlife—it is a law book of cosmic reciprocity. You get there by dying; you get back only by mastering a contract.

Two myths give us the operating manual. Orpheus descends with a lyre and a plea strong enough to move stone and soften rulers of the dead; he wins the right to retrieve Eurydice—on one condition. He fails the condition. The rule is absolute: do not look back. The other manual is Demeter and Persephone: Hades seizes Persephone, Demeter's grief starves the world, and a seasonal compromise is forged. Persephone eats pomegranate seeds—binding food of the dead—and must spend part of each year below. In exchange, the earth rests and rises. The Greek underworld is thus an energy exchange: what is taken returns in rhythms.

What concerns us is the mechanism. Gates, oaths, coins, psychopomps, rules about food, and looking—these are ritual instructions masquerading as narrative. They appear again and again elsewhere. When Greeks initiated re-enacting such journeys in the Eleusinian Mysteries with darkness, chant, and staged revelation, they were not simply watching a play; they were stepping through a workflow meant to change what they believed about dying. Caves—when used—were not scenery; they were instruments. The body moves into constricted stone, the senses are stripped down, the mind generates images and presences— "guides," "judges," "beloved dead." The scene erupts into logos: death is not the end, and the way to make that believable is to *go there and come back.*

B. Hel and Niflhel: The Norse Thresholds Under the Tree

In the Norse cosmos, the universe is a tree (Yggdrasil) and the worlds hang on its roots and branches like nine luminous fruits—Asgard, Midgard, Jötunheim, and lower realms named Hel and Niflhel. Death does not deliver everyone to Odin's mead hall. Those who die of sickness or age go to Hel, ruled by a daughter of Loki whose name is the same as her realm. The path crosses the bridge of Gjöll and the watchful giantess Móðguðr. The landscape is cold, stone-walled, fog-filled. The dead are often said to linger near mounds; doors open at mound-faces; kings receive counsel or weapons from barrow-beings; sorcerers (seiðr) work at the edge of burial and trance. The underworld here is not straightforward punishment; it is a repository of secrets, a place to which the living occasionally travels for knowledge or leverage.

This cosmology embeds descent as politics. Odin himself steals wisdom from below (the runes are first seen as signs of pain and power torn from the tree). Ragnarök—universal winter, wolves devouring the sun and moon, the sea's dead rising—makes Hel not merely a storage for souls but a military reserve. In fragmentary mythic memory, you can still feel the old Indo-European bargain: power is buried; the one who

Psychopomp 101

Everywhere we look we find a "soul-carrier." In Greek tradition, Hermes and Charon are explicit. In Neolithic Southwest Asia and Anatolia, vulture imagery appears to take on this job—birds lifting the soul; heads and circles symbolizing spirit; excarnation as rite.

dares to enter the burial can retrieve it—but not for free. (Late testimonies connect this imagination with older catastrophe stories and apocalyptic winters; we treat those in our other chapters, but note here how the Norse underworld always touches the weather of the world.)

C. Xibalba: The Maya "Place of Fright" and the Black Road

Now pivot to Mesoamerica. The Quiché Maya call their netherworld *Xibalba*— "Place of Fright"—ruled by lords who test and humiliate the living with a carnival of hell-houses: Dark House, Cold House, Razor House, Jaguar House, Bat House. The *Popol Vuh* tells of the Hero Twins who descend to face these trials, suffering defeat and dismemberment before outwitting the powers and returning with authority. Crucially, the road to Xibalba is not only underground. Many Maya artists and scribes represent the entrance as a cave *and* as a corridor in the sky: the Milky Way's Great Rift, sometimes imaged as the jaws of a caiman or a monstrous jaguar. The same sky river that the dead and the sun must travel nightly becomes the "Black Road" (*ri b'e xib'alb'a*). In this sense, the underworld has two addresses—beneath our feet and above our heads—and the myths insist they are the same address viewed from different angles.

In ritual practice, caves and cenotes are physical portals. Here the evidence sings: The Maya left handprints, paintings, incense burners, and "killed" pots (perforated vessels ritually decommissioned) in deep caverns; they performed offerings at watery thresholds where rivers vanish into stone; they built temples that stage thresholds—monster mouths as doorways, serpent bars above lintels, skull racks beyond. The underworld is enacted. And while the Greek contract says "do not look back," the Maya contract says "face the tests." All the same, the structure is familiar: a guide (often owl messengers in the mythic text), a threshold, a series of ordeals, dismemberment, and a rebirth with new powers—the shamanic sequence written as epic.

> **The Black Road in the Sky**
>
> *The Great Rift of the Milky Way—those dark lanes where dust clouds split the starlit river—was read as the road to Xibalba. Caves and monster mouths on earth mirror the caiman's jaws in the sky.*

The Archetypal Descent Journey—and Why It Refuses to Die

Let's name the pattern plainly so we can use it:

1. **Call and Crossing.** Something breaks: a death, a drought, an illness, a command. The hero crosses a threshold (a gate, a river, a cave mouth) into otherness.

2. **Ordeal.** Darkness. Loss of orientation. Tests that unmake identity: don't eat, don't look back, survive jaguars, razors, winter. Often, there is symbolic dismemberment.

3. **Encounter.** A guide arrives (god, ancestor, bird, owl, ferryman). An exchange occurs: a bargain, secret, or initiation.

4. **Return.** Not everyone comes back. Those who do return altered—with new speech (charms), new marks (scarification), new knowledge (how to heal, rule, or sing others across).

Why this rhythm? Because descent is a natural consequence of human neurology in ritual contexts. In deep caves and isolated sanctuaries, light deprivation, carbon-heavy air, rhythmic movement, fasting, and trance techniques democratize visionary experiences that a few spontaneously gifted individuals might otherwise have alone. Communities built frameworks—myths and rituals—to make these experiences legible, repeatable, and useful. The underworld thus becomes a theatre for *learning*, not just a warehouse for the dead.

Cognitive archaeology and ethnography converge on three points:

- **The cave sets the stage.** It is dark, echoic, and physically confining. Sensory monotony plus stress pushes perception toward internally generated imagery—what neurologists call entoptic phenomena: grids, zigzags, tunnels, dots, and pulsations that may then "resolve" into iconic beings and landscapes as the brain tries to interpret them. Ancient artists around the world leave precisely these signatures on rock—sometimes alone, sometimes fused with therianthropes (human-animal combinations), as if the mind stitched geometry to spirit.

- **The initiation is modelled as death.** Ethnographic accounts and prehistoric art repeatedly describe a "breaking down" of the candidate—piercing, dismemberment, skeletonization—and then a rebirth. When re-emerging, initiates describe encounters with beings who teach healing, hunting luck, and weather magic. Caves, with their birth-canal corridors and occasional "womb chambers," reinforce the metaphor: descend to die; ascend to be born.

- **The guide is required.** In many Neolithic and Bronze Age contexts, vultures and other large birds assume this role in art—the psychopomp who carries the head (seat of the soul) or the round "soul" sign westward. In later literature, the role shifts to gods, saints, or angels; the function is stable.

How Myths Become Tools
Underworld stories are not merely beliefs; they are operational protocols. They tell you: who guides you, what to avoid, how to bargain, what to bring back.

There is also a social dimension. Communities police what counts as valid knowledge about origins and the dead. When evidence or experiences don't fit the reigning narrative, institutions tend to ignore or suppress them—as stubbornly in modern disciplines as in ancient priesthoods. This isn't only about fossils or dates; it's about *authority*. The underworld, where the dead and the "first ancestors" dwell, is the ultimate authority—so societies regulate access. Even today, the pattern repeats: anomalous findings that complicate official tales of the past are often minimized; uncomfortable testimony gets edited away. It's the same reflex that makes one culture ban unauthorized oracles and another gatekeep peer review. (We return to this in later parts of your book; for now, note how the descent myth tacitly acknowledges a power source outside the approved pipeline—and then builds an initiation to legitimate it.)

Dismemberment as Curriculum

Why the graphic ordeals? Because they model the breaking of ordinary identity. The initiate becomes "bone"—the universal remainder—so a new person can be built around a different center.

Case Study: Xibalba and the Caves of Belize

You can read about Xibalba all day and still miss the shock of your first step into a Belizean river cave at dusk—the light going blue, bats turning, and the water running cold from a doorway in limestone that looks, unmistakably, like a mouth. The Cayo District and the Vaca Plateau are riddled with cave systems—river tunnels, chambers choked with stalactites, high vaults blackened by ancient smoke. Here, the Maya set out the infrastructure of a working underworld: altars, hearths, pottery caches, and offerings dropped into pools. Archaeologists document pathways of sherds and footprints along slick calcite; ceramic vessels intentionally "killed" (perforated so their "soul" could be released) clustered before stalagmitic formations that were themselves "activated" by hearths and smoke; torch soot permanently matted on ceilings; and human remains in places where the route kinked into a test.

In several Belize caves, you can track a ritual logic in the ground plan:

- **Threshold Pools:** The first chamber is often watery—requiring a wade or swim. Water is both barrier and purifier, an immediate test and rebaptism. The dual nature of Xibalba (death *and* rain, fear *and* fertility) is honoured at once: the offering is to the lords below and to the forces that bring maize. The cave mouth is a maw; the pool is a throat.

- **Processional Routes:** Potsherds, footprints, and torch marks suggest set paths. These lines snake toward rooms of greater darkness and higher acoustic drama. In some caves, formations are arranged almost like congregations facing a central figure or "altar" of calcite.

- **Fire and Breath:** Burnt patches under stalactites, ash lenses, and charred bones imply controlled burnings and incense sessions. Smoke is not incidental: as it rises, drafts carry it into vertical chimneys and out of cracks—the cave "breathes." To participants, this breath is the cave itself responding, and the Old Gods receiving.

- **The Houses of Trial:** Deep chambers re-enact the Popol Vuh's catalogue of ordeals. A frigid, still pool becomes "Cold House." A spine-lined trail along a knife-sharp breakdown becomes "Razor House." A chamber swarming with bats needs no gloss. The experience is curated to mirror the myth—because the myth is the rubric for an education in fear and courage.

The skeletons found in certain Belize caves—adults and adolescents, sometimes calcified to glitter—do not read like random burials. Their placement and accompanying ceramics argue ritual. Scholars debate the balance of sacrifice, fatal accident, and symbolic interment, but no one doubts the cave's role as a door. Once this role is accepted, other details align: the habit of "killing" vessels to release their essence; the arrangement of offerings near stalagmites whose shapes echo maize gods or monster jaws; the repeated matching of subterranean designs to celestial maps—the Great Rift overhead, the caiman's jaws in stars, mirrored by a cavern's mouth below. Here, sky-door and earth-door are one device.

The Hero Twins as an Initiation Syllabus

Reading a Maya Cave: A Field Checklist

Look for: 1) entrance hydrology (is there a pool to cross?); 2) torch soot and ash lenses (ritual frequency, ventilation); 3) "killed" ceramics near striking formations (activation of stone figures); 4) bone placement (route "stations" vs. chambers of culmination); 5) echoes (chants and whistles leave signatures).

Return to the Twins. Their descent through the Houses of Xibalba is not only an epic—it's a stepwise initiation that Belize's ritual routes seem built to emulate: a guided entry (owl messengers; today a priest, elder, or lineage guide), a winnowing series of sensory trials (darkness, cold, animals, blades), and a voluntary "death" from which re-emergence confers healing power and authority. The Twins are dismembered, ground, scattered, and reborn—what many shamans in many places describe as a necessary ordeal. The lesson is not only "do not fear the dead"; it is "become the one who has been there."

Why Bats, Jaguars, and Knives?

Underworld fauna and tools fit the cave ecology and the psyche. Bats are the living presence of the dark. Jaguars are apex fear. Razors and obsidian echo stalactite and flint. Emphasize: the myth's cast is drawn from the cave's own props; that's why it feels inevitable.

What the Belize Caves Teach the Book We're Writing

The book promises what mainstream history "refuses to explain." These caves sharpen that promise. They demonstrate a verifiable pattern of underworld practice that stitches myth, neurology, and stone. They also show another kind of refusal: not ignorance, but discomfort with threshold phenomena that don't stay in their disciplinary lanes. When caves behave like amphitheatres for altered states, we are forced to accept that ancient people engineered consciousness with precision. That is an uncomfortable idea for any paradigm that assumes the past is clever only when it looks like us. The Belize caves prove the opposite: the past is clever exactly when it looks most unlike us—and that difference is the door.

Cross-Comparisons: Hades, Hel, Xibalba—Same Gate, Different Keys

Line up the three traditions, and the same bones show through.

- **Threshold Rule:** Greece: do not look back; do not eat. Norse: pass the gate and its guardian; know the names. Maya: survive the houses; make the right offerings. In all, transgress the rule and you stay below; obey or outwit it and you return with power.

- **Guide Figure:** Hermes/Charon; Móðguðr and barrow-beings; owls and death messengers. The species and gender change; the function does not.

- **Spatial Logic:** Gates cluster at water (Acheron, cenotes), roots (Yggdrasil's wells), and caves. In many cases, the underworld is not entirely below; it is lateral (rivers) and even overhead (the Great Rift). Myth is insisting on an ontology, not a topology: the otherworld is *adjacent* rather than *beneath*.

- **Initiation Use:** Eleusis, mound-sittings, cave trails: they stage controlled descents to produce belief and confer status. By design, participants emerge convinced—because they were made to cross a line, they didn't know they could cross.

- **Economy:** The underworld is not a garbage bin for souls; it is a vault. The living borrows from the dead (knowledge, sanction, fertility, rain) and repays with offerings, oaths, and remembrance.

How to Approach an Underworld Site Without Losing the Plot

If we aim to investigate subterranean worlds that official histories leave unintegrated, we need a disciplined, almost clinical approach:

1. **Start with geology, end with ritual.** Map the cave's hydrology and collapse history; then overlay routes of soot, sherds, and bones. Ritual signatures will likely track natural features that stage an ordeal. (Expect orchestrated crossings at bottlenecks, acoustic "pulpits," and "womb" chambers.)

2. **Audit the ecology of fear.** Bats, darkness, cold, and blade-sharp rock are not incidental; they are the syllabus. Note how offerings cluster around each "lesson."

3. **Listen to the sky.** Chart the site's relation to celestial events and myths—solstices, the Milky Way's position, and local horizon lines. The underworld and the overworld often mirror each other in site planning.

4. **Expect the guide.** In art and placement, something always fulfills the psychopomp role: bird, serpent, deity, or human officiant. If you can't find the guide in imagery, look for it in process—the elder who leads, the song that begins the crossing, the marked staff at the threshold.

5. **Document altered-state engineering.** Darkness durations, drum or rattle tempos, incense types, restricted breathing, fasting regimes—these are the levers. We should catalogue them with the same care we'd map a floor plan. The myth only works because the body was brought to the right brink.

> **Ethics Underground**
>
> *Do not touch calcified remains. Do not move pots. Photograph; measure air and CO_2; leave everything as you found it. Respect local custodians. The underworld belongs to the community that has lived with its mouth in their yard for generations.*

The Descent Pattern in the Present: Why We Still Go Down

If caves taught us anything, it is that descent is not a superstition; it's a human constant. Modern seekers still enter "underworlds"—some literal (spelunking, pilgrimage), some chemical (entheogens), some technological (VR darkrooms, sensory deprivation tanks). The same stages recur: threshold, ordeal, guide, encounter, return with insight or power. Contemporary clinical work with altered states (from trauma therapy to end-of-life care) repurposes the stubborn lesson of the underworld myths: controlled descent heals.

It is tempting to flatten all of this into neurology and declare the matter solved. But that would miss what initiates insist on: whatever the mechanism, the encounter feels *external* and *authoritative*. A pragmatic frame helps: we need not settle whether spirits are "real" to observe that, treated as real, they give real results—courage, healing, social bond, moral law. That is exactly what ancient underworlds delivered: communities that could face death without disintegrating, rulers who claimed legitimacy as those who came back, farmers who believed rain could be convinced to return because someone had a password. Caves trained those convictions into bodies until they felt inevitable.

A Note on Origins and "Buried Realms"

Why do so many cultures—often with no contact—arrive at underworlds with bridges, guardians, birds, rivers, gates, and return rules? Because the topography of descent arises from our shared physiology and environment (caves, darkness, water, fear) and then gets sharpened by inventive ritual. Yet there's a second possibility at the edge of our chapter's remit: that some very old reservoirs of myth and symbol circulated widely—diffused along forgotten routes, catastrophes, and the rebeginning of civilization—and deposited similar images in far places. Comparative work on ancient cosmologies sometimes proposes such deep exchanges. Regardless of how far you take that, the practical upshot is the same: when you meet a cave in a culture's story, expect a doorway and a syllabus.

Stand again at a cave's lip. Hear the water and bat-wings. Imagine the drum and the smoking resin. All three traditions we walked—Greek, Norse, Maya—craft underworlds that refuse to be only metaphors. They are infrastructures of meaning where the living practices the art of dying and returning; where fear is contacted on purpose; where a guide escorts you across, through, and back; where the social world is reminded that its laws lean on older ones. Step inside, and you are in an engineered curriculum: you will be disoriented; you will be tested; you will be shown. Step out, and if you were paying attention, the light will not look the same.

This is how buried realms speak: not in soft voices, but in protocols. The lessons are still valid. The doors are still open.

What Mainstream Narratives Miss

It's not just that myths are beautiful. It's that they encode working methods. The underworld is a machine for turning fear into knowledge. The manuals are still legible. Our job is to read—and to test.

Part II: Subterranean Cities and Lost Civilizations

Chapter 4: The World Below Cappadocia

You don't descend into the ground in Cappadocia so much as slip between eras. The rock exhales cool air, the passage narrows, and suddenly the world above feels provisional—just a brief chapter in a much larger human story written in pumice and silence. This is a landscape where cities learned to breathe through stone, where doors rolled like millstones, where wells doubled as lungs. In this chapter, we go down—together—into the great undergrounds of Derinkuyu and Kaymaklı, we examine their engineering with a clear eye, and we wrestle with a provocative question: were these systems merely "hideouts," or the architectural memory of refugee peoples weathering catastrophe?

Chapter Promise

- *You'll get a tour of Derinkuyu and Kaymaklı that is technical, grounded, and vivid.*
- *We'll unpack how these cities worked—airflow, security, water, food, signaling.*
- *We'll test bold claims against material evidence.*
- *We'll use one case study to evaluate whether "global catastrophe" refugees plausibly shaped this underground world.*

The Stone That Breathes

Cappadocia sits atop stacked ignimbrite—volcanic ash-flow tuffs that set like soft, dry stone after Miocene eruptions. This is the master key. The tuffs carve like firm cheese when freshly exposed, then harden with time as interior surfaces dry, meaning chambers can be dug quickly but remain durable for centuries. This forgiving geology empowered whole communities to move three-dimensionally: to quarry space itself, to pipe air, to shape corridors as choke points, and to nest kitchens beyond smoke's upward will. UNESCO's description of the region is blunt: subterranean cities are part of the same cultural landscape as the rock-cut churches and "fairy chimneys"—it's one integrated building tradition on and below the surface.

Derinkuyu: A City with Lungs

Derinkuyu is the deepest known labyrinth of the region, commonly reported to reach down roughly 85 meters, with a population capacity often estimated at up to twenty thousand souls—including space for animals, food stores, and liturgy. While figures vary in popular accounts, official and scholarly sources converge on its extraordinary depth and complexity.

Inside, you notice what the builders prioritized: air, water, and control of movement. A master ventilation system—dozens of chimneys—threads the whole like organ pipes. One major shaft doubled as a well, engineered to provide water to those below, even if the outside world was dangerous. A meticulous geologic study tallied on the order of fifty-two ventilation chimneys, and documented how floors, walls, and pillars align to manage jointing in the tuff so spaces would neither choke nor collapse.

Security is everywhere. Passages are purposefully low and narrow to slow intruders. Circular "millstone" doors roll across key junctions from the inside; their central apertures work as peepholes or spear-holes, allowing defenders to observe, threaten, or communicate without exposing themselves. Each floor can be sealed independently—modularity avant la lettre—so a breach on one level does not cascade into catastrophe.

The plan is civic, not merely survivalist. You find chapels, a schoolroom with a barrel vault (rare underground), refectories, stables, presses, and storage cells. Archaeology and later memory attest that this space was lived in, not just perched within for an hour of fear.

The Daylight Above: A Rediscovered City

The modern story of Derinkuyu begins with an accident. In the 1960s, a homeowner broke through a basement wall and stared into a tunnel that kept going. It wasn't a rumour for long—media and scholars caught up, and the site opened to the public by the end of that decade. Accounts differ in detail, but independent reporting confirms this serendipitous rediscovery, which kick-started decades of documentation and stabilization.

Kaymaklı: The Broad-Shouldered Sister

If Derinkuyu is depth, Kaymaklı is breadth. Built into eight levels (with four made accessible today), Kaymaklı feels like a town with neighbourhoods—a less vertical, more spread-out plan organized around ventilation shafts. The first level includes a stable and domestic rooms; the second hosts a church with a nave and twin apses; deeper levels concentrate on storage, kitchens, and wine or oil presses. Official materials place Kaymaklı about 20 km from Nevşehir, eight stories deep, with the earliest phase sometimes ascribed to very early periods and subsequent expansions in Roman and Byzantine times.

Local interpretive guides often point out a pitted andesite block with dozens of hemispherical depressions on one of the "industrial" levels, proposing a role in cold-forming copper. The motif appears frequently in visitor literature; the interpretation is intriguing but not yet decisively demonstrated in peer-reviewed work. Treat it as a working hypothesis—and a good example of how living traditions and tourism narratives can race ahead of formal publication.

The Network Instinct (and Its Limits)

You'll hear it said in guidebooks and buses: "These cities are all connected—Kaymaklı to Derinkuyu by tunnels stretching kilometres." It's a thrilling image, a subterranean interstate. And there may be short inter-site links in places. But a careful geotechnical thesis, which measured walls, joints, depths, and shafts, makes a sobering point: despite claims, **there is no conclusive evidence** of a long tunnel directly connecting these two marquee sites. That doesn't mean it never existed; it means we haven't documented it to scholarly standards. For a book committed to both wonder and rigor, that distinction matters.

Kaymaklı–Derinkuyu Tunnel?
Claim vs. Evidence

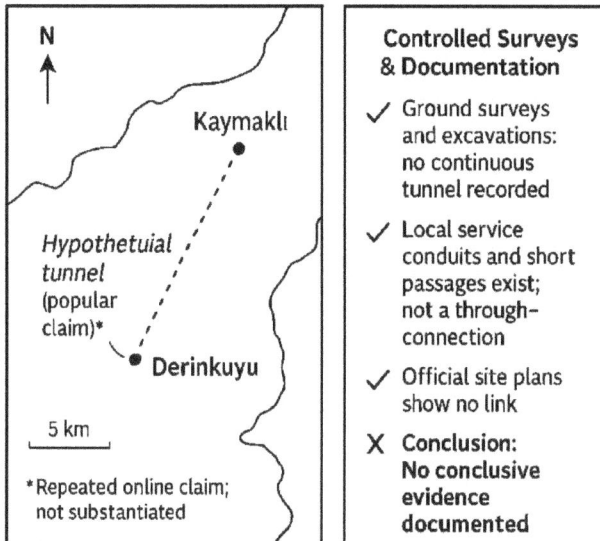

N

Kaymaklı

Hypothetuial tunnel (popular claim)*

Derinkuyu

5 km

*Repeated online claim; not substantiated

Controlled Surveys & Documentation

✓ Ground surveys and excavations: no continuous tunnel recorded

✓ Local service conduits and short passages exist; not a through-connection

✓ Official site plans show no link

X **Conclusion: No conclusive evidence documented**

Air, Fire, Water, Grain: The Engineering You Can Feel

Airflow. The ventilation design is subtle, not just shafts punched upward at random. Diameters vary; some shafts are shared between rooms; some stand apart as quiescent wells when the city is buttoned up. A major shaft at Derinkuyu serves both as a well and as a pressure-management element. The multiplicity of chimneys—on the order of fifty-two—speaks to redundancy against blockage or attack: a living city with fail-safes.

Fire and smoke. Kitchens tend to be deeper, with blackened vaults and minimal cross-breeze that wicks smoke through small, hungry channels rather than roaring draft tubes. Oil and wine presses sit close to storage, limiting the movement of heavy jars in narrow corridors.

Water. Some wells were isolated from the surface so enemies could not poison the supply. Others offered dual access. Hydrology was not an afterthought; it is the city's pulse.

Grain and jars. Kaymaklı's lower levels are punctuated by jar niches and storage rooms—evidence of "economic steadiness" even underground. The implication is resilience planning: the capacity to ride out weeks or longer.

Security architecture. The rolling-stone doors and constricted passages are textbook defensive design. In Özkonak (nearby), small communication/vent holes pierce levels; some are placed so defenders could threaten with spears or pour hot liquids. Even if these latter tactics were occasional or symbolic, they reflect a technology of **controlled contact**—communicate, negotiate, defend—without ceding the corridor.

Four Design Laws Underground

- *Modularity: Sealable floors; breaches are compartmentalized.*
- *Redundancy: Multiple chimneys/wells; alternative routes.*
- *Friction: Corridors slow intruders; force them to stoop; favor defenders.*
- *Proximity: Presses by storage; chapels near dwellings; water near the heart.*

Who Built, Who Used, and When?

The consensus is layered. Earliest cutting may trace to the Iron Age (often attributed to Phrygian traditions), with major expansions in the Roman/Byzantine periods. The **heaviest** documented use as refuge clusters in the Middle Byzantine age, when Arab–Byzantine conflict repeatedly made Cappadocia a frontier. Both archaeological news and regional syntheses point to centuries of intermittent use: from early Christian communities to medieval raids and even up to the early 20th century, when local Greek-speaking families reportedly sheltered underground during periods of violence.

UNESCO embeds Derinkuyu and Kaymaklı in the same listing as the rock-cut churches of Göreme—structurally and historically, they are one cultural fabric.

New Doors Open Underground

Cappadocia continues to surprise. In 2014–2015, a sprawling new complex beneath the Nevşehir fortress was reported—kilometres of tunnels, potentially exceeding Derinkuyu in scale, now under long-term study. Whether that claim holds after full excavation remains to be seen, but the discovery demonstrates that Cappadocia's underground landscape is **still** revealing itself. The ground here is a palimpsest with pages yet unturned.

Case Study: Refugees from a Global Catastrophe?

The Thesis to Test. Could Cappadocia's underground cities be the long shadow of populations seeking sanctuary from a **global** crisis—climatic or otherwise—not just from border raids? If yes, what evidence would we expect to find?

The Historical Spike. Begin with a data point: **AD 536.** Contemporary writers from the Mediterranean world describe a dim sun and a season of cold—the start of what modern climatology calls the **Late Antique Little Ice Age (LALIA)** (ca. 536–660). Ice cores and tree rings support a cluster of massive eruptions in 536, 540, and 547 that depressed Northern Hemisphere temperatures and contributed to harvest failures and disease.

The Regional Context. Cappadocia already sat on a geopolitical fault line. Sasanian incursions, then the Arab–Byzantine wars (7th–10th c.), stressed villages for centuries. Scholarly syntheses on Cappadocian shelters argue that the **most justifiable period of heavy underground expansion** aligns with these raids, not necessarily with a one-off natural event. That is, the **operational** explanation is conflict-driven refuge. But the two frames need not be mutually exclusive: climatic shocks can aggravate conflict, migration, and banditry, multiplying the incentives to burrow.

What We Would Expect If Climate Catalysed Refuge.

1. **Chronology overlap:** More initial cutting and/or deepening near the 6th–7th centuries, not only the periods of later raids.

2. **Provisioning signatures:** Storage capacity scaled for weeks to months; jar-niche density, smoke blackening patterns, soot stratigraphy matching prolonged occupancy.

3. **Water autonomy:** A Greater proportion of below-only wells (no surface access) postdating the mid-6th century.

4. **Population throughput:** Architectural signs of nonlocal usage—ad hoc sleeping bays, mixed cooking hearth designs, sudden expansions.

What the Record Says (So Far)

- **Heavy refuge usage** concentrates in the 7th–11th centuries, where **conflict** is the proximate trigger; this is the mainstream view and is well supported by patterns and finds.
- **LALIA's signal** is strong in the climate archive, but local archaeological coupling to the underground cities is **suggestive**, not definitive. Scholars rightly hesitate to draw a straight causal line from 536 to Cappadocian architecture without stratified evidence.
- **Pragmatic lesson:** The safest reading is **multi-causal**. Climatic stress increases conflict risk and instability; on a frontier like Cappadocia, that's enough to make deep refuge infrastructure rational, even inevitable.

A Balanced Conclusion for the Book. The underground cities are best understood as **security complexes matured under chronic threat**—raids, shifting powers, occasional siege—within a wider Eurasian century-plus of shocks in which climate almost certainly played a background role. That layered context fits the evidence without shrinking the wonder.

Evidence Ladder—
Archaeological Indicators
by Period (Research Framework'k)

	Pre–6th c.	6th–7th c.	7th–11th c.	Post–11th c.
Air shafts count	O	✓	✓	O
Soot layers	✓	✓		O
Jar-niche density	O	✓	✓	O
Well isolation	✓	O	✓	✓
Occupation debris	O	✓	O	✓

✓ Strong indicator

O Weak / preliminary

Hypothetical example –for method illustration only; not a claim.

Benchmark against common evidence matrix /
traffic-light frameworks used in archaeology, CRM, EBM.

The Human Scale: How Life Ran Underground

Dawn belowground. Livestock is fed first; stables sit near the entrance for easier waste removal. Children ferry kindling to deeper kitchens where older women tend gruels that smoke rather than flame. Men rotate to the adits to listen: a stone door never opens cold; it warms first with a whispered exchange through that small round eye.

Sound discipline. Communication pipes—certainly attested at Özkonak—remind us that sound is as essential as oxygen. Short, narrow ducts pass messages floor-to-floor without risking a corridor encounter.

Light economy. Light is precious. Niches mark where oil lamps stood. In some corridors, the walls shine with the polish of shoulders—miner's sheen from centuries of brushing contact.

Faith and memory. Chapels with apses and faint frescos create moral gravity wells. To pray underground is to declare that the city is not only a shelter; it is a polis, a liturgy, a map of the community's obligations.

Myth-Making vs. Material Culture

Let's face it: Cappadocia invites myth. "Megacity," "mystery civilization," "global cataclysm bunkers"—these phrases travel far. But the sites answer back when you listen in stone.

Where myth overreaches:

- **Universal interconnection:** Vast "highways" linking all cities remain unproven; a measured caution is warranted.
- **Extreme antiquity for the deepest levels:** Broad-brush attributions to very remote prehistory drift beyond current evidence. Stratified artifacts and comparative architectural analysis tie the largest expansions to the late Roman and Byzantine centuries.

Where myth aligns with memory:

Practical Life Hacks Underground

- *Stables near the door; kitchens where draft can be tamed.*
- *Storage rooms cluster to minimize jar traffic on steep ramps.*
- *Communication holes reduce corridor risk.*
- *Multi-floor sealing prevents panic spread if one level is breached.*

- **Catastrophe as cultural driver:** Even if a single event cannot explain the digs, human communities **do** respond to layered dangers with layered architectures.
- **A civilization of artisanship:** The quality of ventilation, water isolation, and defensive design reminds us these were not "mere caves," but planned works of communal engineering.

Field Notebook: What to Look For When You Visit

1. **Breathing points.** Find the ventilation shafts. Note their diameters and how rooms are organized around them. Derinkuyu's redundant chimney network is part of its genius.

2. **Security signatures.** Look for door sockets, the rounded edges that let millstones roll, and the little round peepholes.

3. **Water logic.** Trace the relationship between wells and sealed floors—ask guides whether a well connects to the surface or is isolated.

4. **Function mapping.** Identify where food was processed vs. stored; in Kaymaklı, take in how the "industrial" levels sit concerning airflow.

5. **Soot archaeology.** Blackened ceilings tell of sustained use; thin smoke trails near cracks mark mini-drafts.

Visitor's Section Sketch
Field notebook cross-section

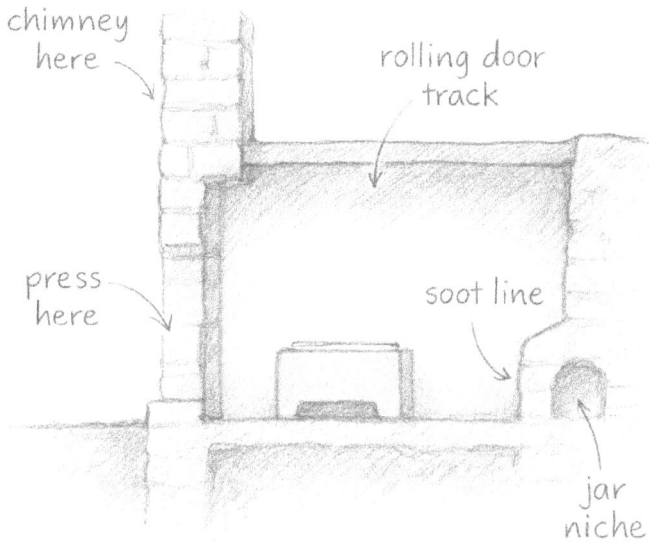

chimney here

rolling door track

press here

soot line

jar niche

Comparative Glance: Özkonak's Talking Stone

Özkonak's reputation rests on its **communication/ventilation drillings** between levels and above entry points. From these, defenders could coordinate, listen, and—so tradition says—pour hot liquids on attackers. Whether or not that last detail was common practice, the architectural intent is clear: **control the vertical conversation**. In comparing sites, you see design diversity: Derinkuyu's depth and redundancy, Kaymaklı's distributed plan, Özkonak's acoustic pragmatism.

Logistics: Feeding Twenty Thousand Under Rock

The oft-quoted "20,000 people" for Derinkuyu pushes us to ask hard questions: grain tonnage, lamp oil, livestock waste, and air exchange rates. Even if that figure reflects a **surge capacity** rather than a stable census, the provisioning architecture supports **multi-week endurance**:

- **Storage:** Rows of jar niches and storage rooms indicate planned stockpiling; in Kaymaklı, the sheer surface area devoted to storage on lower levels is striking.

- **Air:** A network with ~52 chimneys in Derinkuyu suggests distributed intake and exhaust—less risk of a single choke point.

- **Water:** Isolated wells mean less dependence on surface conditions.

- **Traffic:** Narrow ramps limit throughput—good for defence, bad for panic. The city's design reflects a **shelter-in-place logic**, not frequent large-scale circulation.

A Living Scholarly Conversation

Archaeology in Cappadocia is ongoing; we should expect revisions. A rigorous thesis from Middle East Technical University highlights that floor depths, shaft counts, and even total areal coverage still carry uncertainties due to reference-level choices (are you measuring to the bottom of a ventilation shaft, a water shaft, or the last habitable floor?). That same study reminds us that **what sounds simple in a guidebook can be technically fraught in the rock.**

On the cultural history side, leading syntheses put the most intense period of digging and usage during the Arab–Byzantine centuries; encyclopaedic overviews on Cappadocia corroborate that long-run pressure landscape. Meanwhile, climate historians assemble the 6th-century "year without a proper sun" from ice cores and tree rings. The intersection of these strands—conflict and climate—will remain a fruitful space for research.

Wonder But with Handrails

Standing in a carved chapel on the second floor of Kaymaklı, you may feel a sudden rush: the sound of feet above, a rush of cool air, a murmur through a comms hole you can't see. In such places, myth is not the enemy—**imprecision** is. Cappadocia's underground cities are marvels of human adaptation, not just because they are big, but because they are **wise**: the wisdom of redundancy, of modular defence, of faith integrated with logistics, of communities that learned to **shape time** by shaping stone.

If you carry one thing out of this chapter, take this: the world below Cappadocia is not simply an escape hatch. It is an **architecture of continuity**, a civilization strategy pressed into ignimbrite—built by hands who expected the unexpected, whether it came as a border raid, a bad harvest, a dim sun, or all at once.

Chapter 5

The Labyrinths of Egypt

D awn licks the desert with a thin spill of apricot light as we step off the asphalt and onto the Fayum's wind-combed crust. The oasis haze hangs low, a silver veil over fields coaxed green by canals that inherit the ancient name of a vanished lake—Moeris. Beneath this quiet, the ground remembers something vast: halls that once swallowed kings and confounded conquerors, corridors that bent time into ritual, and vaults that, even now, rumour-stocked, are said to hold maps of the underworld. We are hunting a legend that refused to die—the Egyptian labyrinth.

Come with me as co-investigator, boots dusty, notebook open. We'll braid myth with measurement, rumour with excavation, and ask a simple question with complicated consequences: what did Egypt bury—and why?

The Memory Palace by the Lake

When Greek travellers reached Egypt, they were not easily impressed. Yet one of them left with his astonishment intact. He wrote of a building near the mouth of a great lake, with twelve courts and "unending" rooms, more wondrous than the pyramids themselves. He was told there were thousands of chambers—some above, some below—and that the lower halls held the tombs of kings and sacred crocodiles. He walked the upper levels, he said, but was barred from the subterranean ones. Whether or not every detail survived accurately in translation and retelling, the punchline did: the Egyptians had built a maze to humble memory.

Today, we anchor that report to a place: Hawara, at the southeast corner of the ancient Fayum. Here, a 12th-Dynasty pharaoh—celebrated as Africa's great water engineer—raised his pyramid and, scholars broadly agree, a colossal adjacent mortuary complex. The pyramid's masonry is battered to a core; its temple—if we strip away later quarrying, earthquakes, and reuse—dissolves into a confusion of foundations. But in the sand we still read traces: massive bedding platforms, dense grids of walls, and the suggestion of a plan whose ambition was administrative, religious, and cosmic at once.

The labyrinth was not just a building. It was a statement. It said: order can be built from flood and silt; the state can organize chaos; the path through life and death has a plan.

What Makes a Labyrinth Egyptian?

The word "labyrinth" pulls our minds toward Greek myth: a bull-headed monster, a hero with a thread. Egypt, though, made labyrinths with a different grammar. In Egypt, mazes are not puzzles—they are processions. The Egyptians loved sequences: hours of the night, gates of the Duat (the netherworld), lists of nomes (districts), ranks of deities, and protocols for purification. Their funerary books chart narrow corridors through cosmic geography; their temple walls choreograph movement with pylons and courts. The labyrinth at Hawara, as described, reads like that writ in stone: 12 courts (think: 12 months, 12 hours, 12 divisions), innumerable rooms (think: the serial rooms of purification), an above-world for the living and a below-world for the dead.

Egyptian labyrinths aren't games; they are ceremonial circuits.
- *Purpose: to rehearse, structure, and sanctify passage—across districts, ranks, or the hours of night.*
- *Form: serial courts, processional corridors, controlled thresholds; an "above ground" for administration and ritual, a "below ground" for tombs and sancta.*
- *Meaning: a civic-and-cosmic filing system—where governance, theology, and afterlife logistics converge.*

Call it an architecture of rehearsal. You processed through order so that the order would process through you.

Herodotus and the Lost Building

Let's reconstruct sensibly. The author whose report we channel visited in the fifth century BCE, long after the 12th Dynasty (c. 19th century BCE), but still within an Egypt that curated its past. If he saw twelve courts, a massive stone roof, and "endless" rooms, he wasn't describing a ruin heap—he described continuity. That implies that in the Late Period, the Hawara complex (or a successor structure at the Fayum's edge) still stood in legible form. The prohibitions he met—no access to the subterranean halls—fit Egyptian sacral zoning: lower chambers were often cultic, restricted, and integrated with embalming or mortuary mystery rites.

When he compared the labyrinth to the pyramids and preferred the former, he was measuring not just stone tonnage but experience: pyramids stun from the outside; labyrinths swallow you whole.

The Ground Beneath the Sphinx

Shift north to the limestone plateau of Giza, where the Great Sphinx reclines like a geological dream partially awake. If Egypt harbors an underground imagination, Giza is its poster child. For generations, local tales and occasional tantalizing finds have suggested hollows beneath the paws and flanks—voids, shafts, and bedrock fissures charted by rainwater and human chisels alike. Survey instruments— seismic, resistivity, ground-penetrating radar—have, at various times, reported anomalies: discreet cavities; linear features that look conspicuously unnatural; pits with water seeping into deeper levels.

Some are well attested and uncontroversial. A multi-level shaft complex west of the Great Pyramid drops through chambers with niches and granite coffers, reached today by stair and pontoon when the water table rises. Scattered mastabas conceal further shafts and side rooms, an anthill of Old Kingdom ambition. Other "tunnels"—especially those that claim grand, continuous corridors connecting the Sphinx to pyramids or secret libraries—remain more rumour than record, embroidered by misread surveys, misattributed photographs, or the very human habit of turning "a cavity here" and "a passage there" into a single mighty legend underground.

Our job isn't to take everything literally; it's to peel literalism back to the human need beneath it. Giza's substructures—whatever their limits—do demonstrate a cultural comfort with *down*. The Egyptians didn't locate all their holiness in the sky; they carved some of it into bedrock.

Eyewitness hierarchies of wonder: Why a labyrinth could eclipse a pyramid in antiquity.

- *Pyramids = monumentality + celestial alignment.*
- *Labyrinth = scale + complexity + participation; it makes you move and submit to a sequence.*
- *Cultural echo: processional architecture may have "felt" more sacred to visitors than inert bulk.*

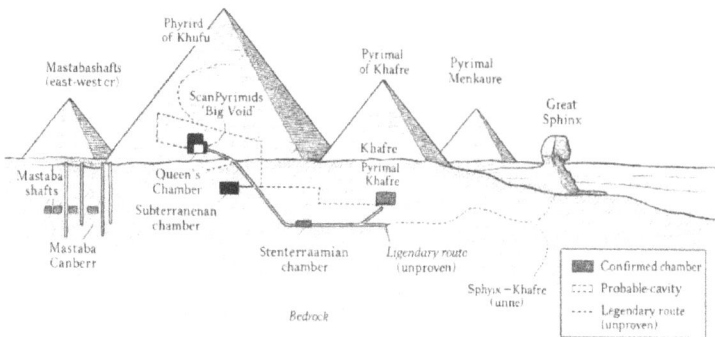

GIZA PLATEAU: CONFIRMED CHAMBERS AND SURVEYED ANOMALIES
(CUTAWAY 2025)

Hawara: Where the Labyrinth Touches the Shovel

Return to the Fayum. Here, wind has unstitched masonry into low platforms, the irrigation map has migrated, and modern villages nestle against ancient mounds. You stand on a vast floor of laid stone and broken walls like ribs—this is where the "lost labyrinth" becomes dirt and tool.

The pyramid at Hawara, built for the 12th-Dynasty king Amenemhat III, once wore fine limestone; its guts are a tough, reworked stone core. The associated temple, conventionally identified with the labyrinth's "upper world," sprawled beside it. Early archaeological work here mapped alignments, counted column bases, and followed wall lines until they melted into the pit dug for later blocks. Surprise: those blocks got recycled everywhere—from nearby towns to Roman-period buildings across the region. A complex that once housed a court, cult, and maybe archives became a quarry.

But ruins have long memories. Even in the partial map, patterns whisper: courts aligned along axes; side-rooms in serial ranks; thresholds thickened like dams to control traffic; column forests that would have registered, to a human body, as both overwhelming and navigable—if you knew the order.

In recent decades, geophysical surveys—noninvasive peeks into the ground—have lit up the area around the pyramid with rectilinear signatures. Some teams saw a "grid" that looked like rooms; others cautioned that saturated soils and modern agriculture complicate readings. Excavation is slow. Sand keeps its secrets until money, permits, and politics align.

So, we move carefully, but we move—and we keep the space open for real surprise.

> *What's real under Giza—and what's likely a story.*
> - *Real: Vertical shafts with multiple chambers; sealed bedrock niches; water-filled lower levels; short connecting passages; causeway substructures.*
> - *Unproven/Exaggerated: One continuous "library tunnel" linking Sphinx and pyramids; vast walkable corridors spanning the whole plateau; undisturbed palace-sized vaults beneath the paws.*

Why Here? The Water, the Crocodile, and the Crown

The Fayum is Egypt's engineered miracle. An ancient canal—the Bahr Yussef—leads Nile water westward into a natural depression, creating a lake that waxed and waned with royal will. To tame a flood is to mimic a god. Amenemhat III's waterworks were feats of hydraulic control, and the labyrinth can be read as their ritual counterpart: a civic machine to organize people as canals organized water.

Crocodiles, late in Egyptian religion, wore crowns and jewellery in this region. Sobek, the crocodile god, enjoyed special devotion in the Fayum: power, fertility, the bite of kingship. Sacred crocodiles embalmed and installed in subterranean galleries made literal one Greek traveller's line: tombs of crocodiles below. Here, the labyrinth's "lower halls" lock onto cult practice, not fantasy.

This is Egypt at its most integrated: waterscape, kingship, and architecture weaving a narrative of control—the state shaping the flood, the temple shaping the state, the labyrinth shaping the human procession through both.

Rumors of Tunnels: Mapping the Psychology

Sobek and the State: why crocodiles matter at Hawara.

- *Sobek's attributes: strength, fertility, protection of the king.*
- *Fayum cult centers: crocodile burials and lakeside sanctuaries.*
- *Labyrinth logic: processional order upstairs; sacred zoology and embalming below—two halves of one ritual economy.*

Why do subterranean rumours cling to the Sphinx and Hawara alike? Because Egypt teaches that truth comes in layers. Tombs hide within cliffs; serdabs hide statues behind false doors; Osiris rules a realm beneath the western horizon. The culture codified *secrecy*: not to deceive but to instruct—only the prepared pass the gate.

We, moderns, mistake a teaching device for a conspiracy. Of course, there are chambers we haven't opened; of course, there are passages we haven't traced. But the real "secret" is not a library in a vault; it's the blueprint embedded in Egyptian ritual thought: you compose the world by moving through it along an ordained path. The labyrinth is a pedagogical machine.

The real secret of Egyptian "tunnels."

It isn't what is hidden but how you move: passage as initiation, order as revelation. The labyrinth is a training ground for the mind that will meet the Duat.

Case Study: Reading the Hawara Complex from the Ground Up

L et's reconstruct an experience, informed by archaeology and ritual logic.

You approach from the canal on a causeway elevated above fields. Ahead, the pyramid shoulders up from the plain, its casing long vanished. To the right spreads a rectangular precinct—our labyrinth—ringed with walls. You pass through a monumental gate into the first court: sunlight, echo, the smell of dust and stone. Officials here once received delegations, sorted petitions, and marshalled processions. You continue, court to court, your route bending like a meander, each threshold narrowing the crowd until only select bodies remain for the inner rites.

Columns thicken. Ceilings weigh down. Light is rationed. Scenes on walls (now mostly gone, once painted) would have narrated offerings, enthronements, rituals of foundation and renewal. Somewhere, a stair or ramp dives down; access is denied to many. Below, in cool chambers, embalmers and priests of Sobek tend to sacred bodies; elsewhere, a king's closed tomb or cenotaph anchors the complex's claim to eternity. The roar of a crowd above fades into the lapping of dark water below.

You re-emerge, not lost but *led*.

A likely sequence of experience at Hawara:
1. *Canal-side approach: procession begins.*
2. *Outer courts: administration and assembly.*
3. *Inner halls: ritual concentration.*
4. *Restricted descent: embalming, burial, secrecy.*
5. *Exit back to light: renewal and return.*

The Labyrinth as Archive

Egypt's memory is administrative. Lists of taxes, deliveries of grain, rosters of labor brigades, inventories of offerings—these made the state breathe. Imagine portions of the Hawara labyrinth as a living archive: scribal rooms arranged by nome or season, chambers whose contents rotated with the flood calendar, storerooms recording redistribution of fish, flax, papyrus, and oil. In this light, the "thousands of rooms" are less a marvel of confusion than a masterwork of filing. The labyrinth is bureaucracy consecrated.

And because in Egypt the sacred and the civic are Siamese twins, you cannot tease one from the other: record-keeping upstairs paired with intercession downstairs; grain tablets paired with crocodile mummies; royal jubilees paired with crocodile processions. The labyrinth is a hinge.

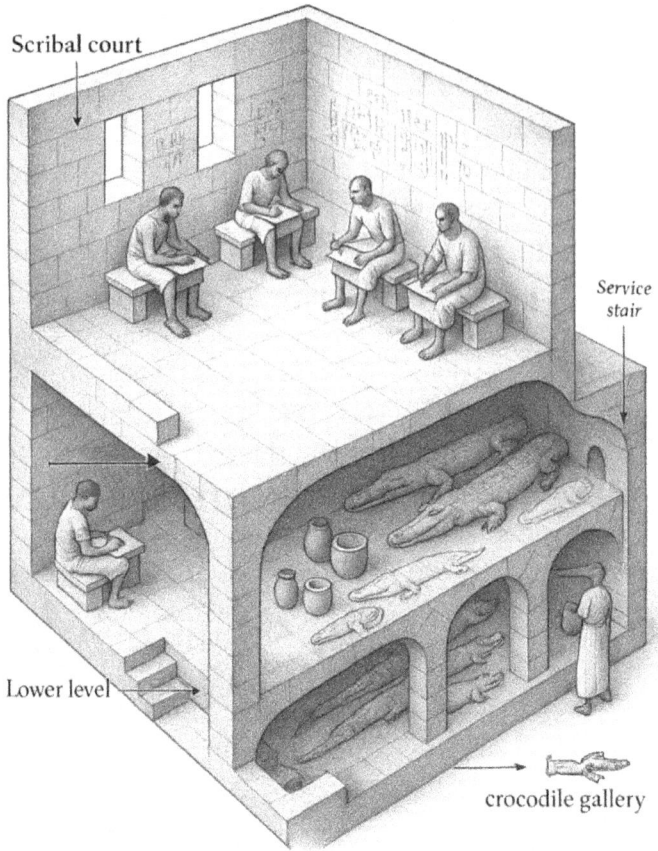

Two floors, two functions, one sacred economy

Hypothetical reconstruction based on Herodotus (II.14 88–149),
Strabo (17.1.37), Petrie (1890) plan at Hawara; lower level
crocodile gallery inspired by Tebtunis catacombss (Fayum).

Methods: How We Know What We Know

Being human about evidence means keeping our excitement tethered
to method. Here's our toolbox when dealing with buried labyrinths:

- **Archaeological mapping:** even fragmentary wall lines plot
  pathways. Measure axes, module sizes, and doorway widths to
  infer movement and control.

- **Geo-survey (GPR, seismic, resistivity):** useful for spotting voids, thick walls, and moisture pockets—but always ground-truth with excavation where possible.

- **Hydrological context:** model ancient lake and canal levels; understand how water tables shift to interpret submerged rooms.

- **Comparative ritual architecture:** read parallels in other Middle Kingdom mortuary temples to reconstruct lost functions.

- **Stratigraphy and reuse:** track quarry scars, breakage patterns, and Roman/medieval re-appropriations to reverse-engineer what once stood.

Egypt's Labyrinth Mindset Beyond Hawara

When we widen our lens, labyrinth-thinking appears across Egypt:

- **Valley of the Kings:** A topography of secret, twisting tombs carved into Theban cliffs—labyrinthine by intent, designed to foil both robbers and the unprepared spirit.

- **Temple complexes (Karnak, Luxor):** Layered pylons and courtyards that choreograph the feast calendar—pilgrims proceed through gates as if threading a maze of meaning.

- **Catacomb galleries (Crocodilopolis, Tuna el-Gebel):** Long, low corridors with niches upon niches, sacred animals installed in an unending series—ritual storage as a labyrinth.

Hawara isn't an isolated anomaly; it's the apex of an instinct: the architecture of sequence.

Skeptic, Believer, Investigator

Where should our needle settle between an ardent believer in sprawling underground cities and an austere skeptic who sees only rubble? The honest place is in the middle, with boots on the ground. We acknowledge: there are real multi-level shafts, real restricted chambers, real substructures that justify the durable rumour that "Egypt is hollow." We also acknowledge: the human appetite for secrets inflates cavities into continents.

So we adopt a humility suited to labyrinths: we proceed step by step. We hold two truths at once: (1) much remains unexcavated; (2) not every anomaly will bloom into a revelation. And we keep our curiosity sharp.

Ground-Truthing the Anomaly

Anomaly, meet archaeology.

Sidebar Inquiry: Could the Labyrinth Encode the Duat?

Egypt's netherworld books (Amduat, Book of Gates) divide the night into hours, each with gates, guardians, and challenges. What if the Hawara labyrinth—its twelve courts, its graded thresholds—mirrored those passages? A visitor, walking in daylight, rehearsed the soul's night journey. The king's eternal passage below found its echo above in civilian processions, state festivals, and training rituals.

This reading doesn't require a single "master key room" or stash of forbidden texts. It asks us to see the building as a living *commentary*—you don't read it; you *walk* it.

Field Notes from Hawara Today

Stand at midday on the wind-fretted stone. Local children trace bicycle tracks across the past. A shepherd leans into the shade. The pyramid's jagged heart broods against the sky. Between your boots, small things: a scrap of polished limestone, a fleck of pigment, a potsherd rim. The labyrinth is more absent than present now, yet you *feel* the order, like a muscle memory of the ground. This is how buried realms talk to those who listen: not with trumpets but with alignments.

Practical Intelligence: How to Investigate Legends Without Getting Lost

1. **Start with the oldest descriptions—but interrogate them.** What could a foreign visitor misread? What would a priest permit him to see?

2. **Anchor legends to sites with multiple lines of evidence.** Can you plot the story on a map? Do the ruins' footprints nod along?

3. **Separate *existence* claims from *extent* claims.** A chamber may exist; its alleged miles-long reach may not.

4. **Honor local knowledge.** Folklore remembers outlines; archaeology fills in anatomy.

5. **Beware the binary.** "All hoax" and "all true" are lazy choices. Most buried stories are mixed tapes.

Community-Informed Fieldwork Cycle

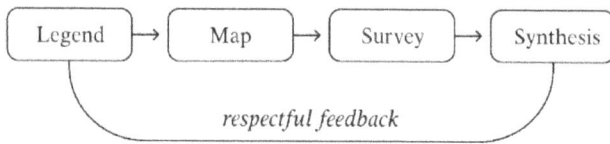

Community-Informed Fieldwork Cycle

The Labyrinth, the Sphinx, and the Human Brain

One more thread: labyrinths are externalized cognition. They are how a culture thinks in stone. Egypt, obsessed with balance—Ma'at—built machines to enforce sequence, to domesticate flood-time and night-time alike. The Sphinx watches the horizon; the labyrinth encodes the route. Together, they are diagrams of attention: look outward to stars, move inward through gates. It's no accident that modern brains, encountering these forms, dream of secret tunnels. The form invites the dream.

A Measured Vision Forward

What should we ask of the next decade at Hawara and Giza?

- **Targeted trenches informed by high-resolution surveys** at Hawara's suspected "pivot" zones—where processional routes bend and meet.

- **Hydrological stabilization and underwater archaeology protocols** for lower chambers, acknowledging a rising water table and protecting fragile deposits.

- **Materials analysis of recycled blocks** in surrounding villages and later temples to virtually "reassemble" portions of the labyrinth.

- **Open-data publication pipelines**—plans, scans, and trench diaries—so global scholarship can iterate reconstructions responsibly.

- **Public storytelling that respects mystery without minting myth,** so curiosity is fed, not fooled.

Through the Maze, Toward the Light

We came in search of a building and found a worldview. Egypt's labyrinth is not lost; it's distributed among foundations at Hawara, shafts at Giza, scrolls of the Duat, and the rituals that taught a people to walk their cosmos in order. The rumor of tunnels persists because, in a way, it's true: Egypt tunnelled through time, not merely the ground.

So, we leave this chapter where labyrinths always leave us: back at the entrance, but not the same. The map we carry out is not a floor plan; it's a discipline—curiosity harnessed to method; wonder braided to evidence. That is how buried realms yield to us, one measured turn at a time.

Chapter 6:

The Caves of the Americas

There are places in the Americas where the ground does not simply hold you up—it speaks to you. Canyons that breathe, caves that drink rivers and give them back as cold blue springs, tunnels where sound behaves oddly, and the air itself feels older than history. Step into one of these apertures and the ordinary world blurs at the edges. The ancients said such places are doors. Modern science says they are karst systems, pressure gradients, resonant chambers, ancient aquifers, and geologic time folded into limestone. Both may be right.

This chapter is our descent rope. We'll follow the stories into the dark—Hopi emergence traditions, the Grand Canyon's "forbidden caves," and the most notorious article ever printed about a cavern in Arizona—then climb back out with context, fieldcraft, and a clear eye for evidence. You and I will co-investigate every claim, hold myth and measurement in each hand, and listen for the deeper rhythm that makes caves a universal stage for origin stories, initiations, and the occasional hoax.

The American Cave Mindset: Why portals keep reappearing

Across the Americas, caves are more than shelters; they are thresholds. Ethnographies from the Arctic to the Andes keep returning to the same choreography: isolation, darkness, a feeling of being "drawn down," visions that blur geometric lattices into beings, and then a return—initiated, changed, bearing medicine or knowledge. In many traditions, the initiate enters a hidden opening that "wasn't there before," a mouth in a cliff that opens only to the chosen, and must seize the instant to leave, or remain "shut up in the cave forever." The cave is a concrete symbol of descent, death, and re-emergence into a wider order of knowing.

These patterns aren't confined to a single person or period. Mesoamerican cosmology, for instance, locates a watery underworld accessible through cave mouths—portals to a realm of trials and transformations, sometimes depicted with night-jungle beasts and pitch-black pools that stand for death and renewal. Rock art and ritual architecture echo the same grammar: tunnels as wombs, chambers as bellies, handprints and lattices as the moment where mind meets stone. Mythic language, neuropsychology, and archaeology converge in these deep, dark spaces.

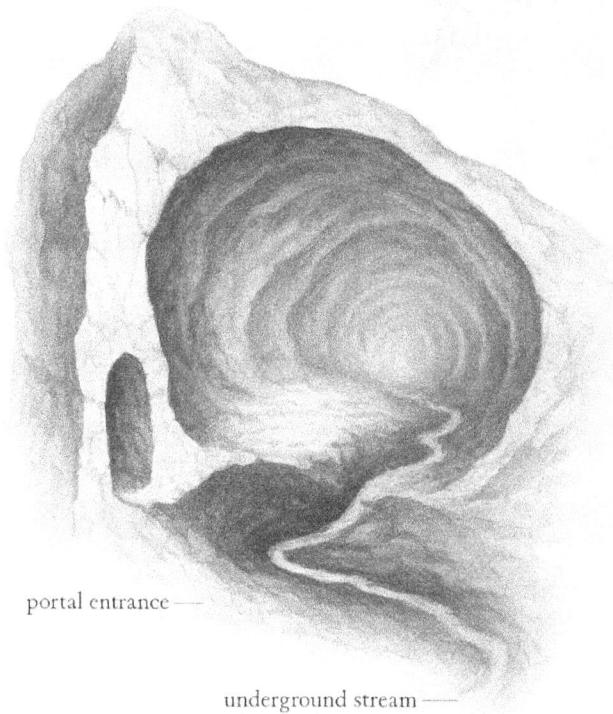

portal entrance ——

underground stream ——

Resonant Karst Sanctuary

Hopi Legends of Emergence from the Underworld

Ask the Hopi where we came from and some will point toward the confluence of the Little Colorado and Colorado rivers—a place they know as **Sipapuni**, the "place of emergence." The landscape helps you believe it: travertine domes, mineral-rich water the color of a robin's egg, and the canyon's furnace-light folded into turquoise shade. In Hopi memory, ancestors traveled upward from a prior world through a cosmic passage, emerging here into the Fourth World to begin the long work of walking and learning under the guidance of the earth-lord and spirit keeper of this world.

The route into this moral geography isn't just a story; it's walked. The **Hopi Salt Trail** descends Little Colorado's walls to sacred salt beds and passes near the emergence area, threading pilgrimage and ecology into one embodied rite. To walk it properly is to rehearse the cycle—descent, acquisition, return—with the canyon itself as teacher.

What's striking, besides the beauty, is the grammar of the myth: descent through a narrow opening; a watery, perilous zone between worlds; emergence into responsibility. The motif is Pan-American—northern Plains traditions speak of peoples living "in a large village underground" with a vine or opening to the surface, a story scholars have long read as memory filtered through symbol. The point is ethical as much as historical: you don't just arrive; you **earn** the surface.

Sipapuni: What the Place Teaches

Treat Sipapuni not as "a location to bag," but as a living node in Hopi cosmology. It encodes obligations: humility in descent, restraint at the source, gratitude in return. Respect means distances kept, permits honored, and stories listened to, not extracted.

The Grand Canyon "Forbidden Caves" Mystery

You'll hear it in gathering places and on late-night channels: the Canyon hides a "forbidden zone" packed with secret caves—some lethal, some sacred, some sealed by conspirators. Part of this is romance; part is policy. The National Park Service's current guidance is simple: **Grand Canyon caves are closed to public visitation except for research.** There are good reasons—hazards, fragile speleothems, endangered bats, archaeological integrity, and, critically, the protection of living tribal cultural landscapes. "Forbidden," in other words, is not a mystic ban word; it's a practical shield.

Equally important: "Forbidden Zone" is **not** an official designation. It's a tourism-and-internet coinage that blurs genuine closures, sovereign tribal lands, and seasonal restrictions into a single melodramatic phrase. If you encounter the term, translate it into: "off-limits for safety, science, or sovereignty."

What "Closed" Really Means in the Canyon

- *Caves: closed to the public; research permits only.*
- *Certain areas: closed to protect resources or for seasonal hazards; tribal lands require tribal permission.*
- *"Forbidden Zone": pop-culture term; always check NPS and tribal policies instead of rumor.*

HOW CAVE ACCESS ACTUALLY WORKS:
RESEARCH-ONLY CAVES, SEASONAL AREA CLOSURES & TRIBAL LANDS (PERMITS)

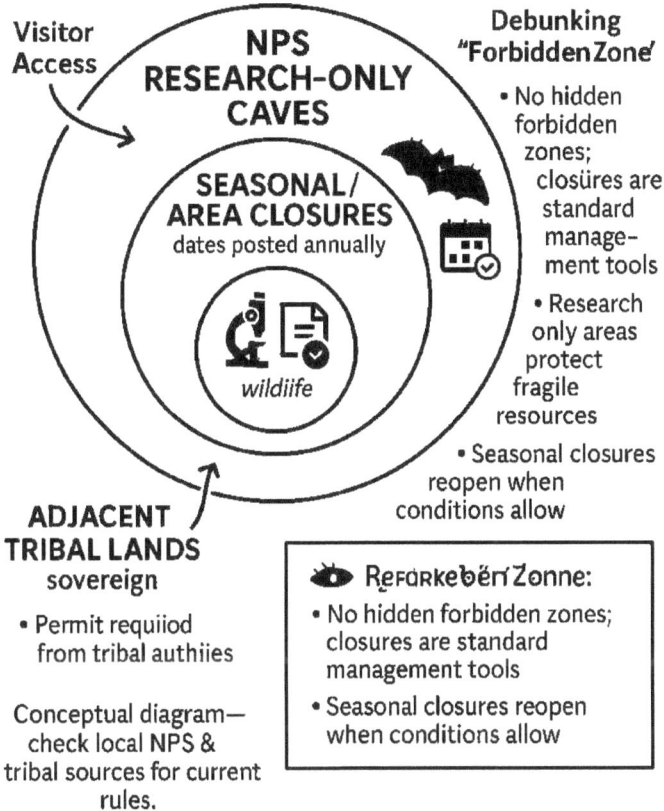

Visitor Access

NPS RESEARCH-ONLY CAVES

SEASONAL/ AREA CLOSURES
dates posted annually

wildlife

Debunking "Forbidden Zone"

- No hidden forbidden zones; closures are standard management tools

- Research only areas protect fragile resources

- Seasonal closures reopen when conditions allow

ADJACENT TRIBAL LANDS
sovereign

- Permit requiiod from tribal authiies

Conceptual diagram— check local NPS & tribal sources for current rules.

RefORkebërïZonne:
- No hidden forbidden zones; closures are standard management tools
- Seasonal closures reopen when conditions allow

Case Study: The 1909 Phoenix Gazette Report of Egyptian Artifacts in Arizona

No story casts a longer shadow over Canyon lore than the *Arizona (Phoenix) Gazette* front-page splash of **April 5, 1909**. The article claimed that an explorer had found a cavern city carved into rock—mummies, hieroglyph-like inscriptions, statues—immediately tied to a supposed Smithsonian professor and, by implication, to ancient Egypt or Tibet. It's a heck of a tale—and nearly all modern retellings boil back to this single newspaper text.

How the legend was built

The piece is vivid: a hidden entrance, a labyrinth of chambers "for 50,000 people," artifacts with supposed "Oriental" traits, and expert sponsorship. It is also a specimen of its time—an era when American papers regularly printed serial hoaxes, and when the Canyon itself was a stage for boosterism, land politics, and wonder-mongering. Later write-ups repeated the claims, mixed in new names, and wrapped the whole in a cloak of institutional cover-up. But when the dust settled, no verifiable field notes, maps, artifact photographs, or provenanced materials ever surfaced from a credible archive.

What the record shows

Independent historians, Canyon archivists, and librarians have searched for the expedition's supposed principals, for the promised collections, for any Smithsonian accession numbers. The result? **No Smithsonian records** of the named individuals or any such expedition; no catalog entries for the alleged artifacts; no follow-up science of the sort a discovery of this magnitude would have triggered. When archivists checked again in modern times, the ledger stayed blank.

Why it persists

The tale endures because it lives in a perfect fuel-mix: the Canyon's thousand-plus caves (most little studied), genuine closures that outsiders label "forbidden," and our hunger for a lost chapter that flips the script on "who got where first." But persistent isn't the same as persuasive. A single century-old feature story, without subsequently verifiable data, does not meet even a relaxed evidentiary threshold.

LEGEND VS. LEDGER:
A PROVENANCE GAP

How to Read the 1909 Story like a Researcher

- *Primary vs. derivative: nearly all modern articles trace back to one newspaper piece.*
- *Archival check: verify museum/Smithsonian accessions; none exist.*
- *Field correlates: exact cave location, maps, measured drawings, artifact photos; none verified.*
- *Conclusion: compelling folklore, not established archaeology.*

Beyond Arizona: Initiation caves and underworlds from Mesoamerica to the Sub-Arctic

If you widen the map, the cave-as-portal pattern becomes even harder to ignore. In Central America, a "Place of Fright" underworld is entered through cave mouths and water tunnels; its houses—the Dark House, Jaguar House, Razor House—are not just obstacles but initiatory classrooms. In art, underworld guides appear as part-animal, part-human beings; in caves, negative handprints and entoptic motifs spiral and grid across stone as if a vision left fingerprints. The motif stretches north as well: vision quests in cliff caves; healing "ghost ceremonies" that simulate death and return; initiates pierced or dismembered in trance and then "reborn." Different languages, same dramaturgy.

And always the environment collaborates. Deep chambers with black pools become liminal pools; echo-rich galleries double as spirit haunts; tight fissures force bodily humility before intellectual humility can bloom. Cave, rite, and story synthesize into a living technology for changing human beings.

"Forbidden Caves" and Sacred Geography: The ethics of looking

One reason closures inflame imaginations is that they hide their reasons poorly: bats do not tweet press releases; ancestral sites do not lobby. Yet the reasons are tangible. Cave ecosystems shatter easily—one boot on a guano bank can collapse a maternity colony's season. Foot oil kills calcite growth that took centuries. And in the Canyon, closures often protect **living** relationships between people and place, not museum relics. If we're truly curious, curiosity must be paired with consent.

Anomalies in the Vault: When caves collide with chronology

If the Gazette tale withers under scrutiny, other cave stories complicate the tidy timelines. In the mid- to late-20th century, controversies erupted around cave contexts in North America that seemed **too old**. A uranium-series date on a stalagmite layer sealing cultural material in a New Mexico cave was discussed at roughly a quarter-million years— wildly earlier than orthodox models for fully modern humans in the Americas. Elsewhere, leaf-shaped points and hearths under travertine spurred disputes about rodent burrowing versus in-place deposition. In California, deep mine tunnels into ancient gravels produced worked stone that many thought impossible at such ages. Some researchers accepted one anomaly while rejecting another; critics charged methodological inconsistency; the debates never entirely died.

What should we, as careful investigators, make of this? First, that **context is king** in caves. Limestone breathes; water moves; animals move artifacts; calcite grows irregularly. Radiometric clocks tick inside mineral matrices but must be interpreted with stratigraphic sobriety. Second, that even when dates are re-evaluated downward—or rejected—caves remain places where chronology is both opportunity and trap. They preserve beautifully. They also trick us. The work is to let them **teach** us, not merely confirm us.

The Grand Canyon's Blue Rooms: Water, sound, and initiation

Return to the Canyon and imagine you're standing at the lip of a tunnel where rushing water drowns speech. In the darkness, the sides of a "vortex" seem gridded, as if you are being pulled through a rotating threaded tube. Many initiates report exactly this sensation as trance deepens: a descent through a tunnel lined by flickering squares that soon overlay with animals and beings. It's not hard to see how such inner imagery would find, in real caves and galleries, the perfect outer screen. Place and perception co-author the experience.

In some canyons, a black pool down in a chamber is narrated as a literal entrance to the realm of death and transformation. Caves with water aren't just geologic—they are pedagogic. The message isn't "fear the void," but "embrace the cycle": death, dismemberment, reassembly, return. The subterranean is where you learn to carry power safely.

Myth, Memory, and the Other Americas

Listen widely enough and the Americas are full of upward stories—emergences from caves, lakes, and "subterranean villages." Some northern traditions even preserve a vine-or-rope motif by which the first people climbed to the light, only for the passage to break and strand those below—a poignant image of separation written in vines rather than stone. These are not travelogues; they are moral cartographies, instructing each generation how to move through peril and hunger without losing shape.

The resonance with other hemispheres is not an argument for one-to-one diffusion so much as evidence that **human beings, everywhere, use holes in the earth to talk about thresholds in the soul.** When people need to teach endurance, humility, service, and the art of return, a cave says it cleanly: narrow entrance, long night, first light.

The Grand Canyon, Re-seen

So where does our descent leave us? With a Cave Canon, of sorts:

1. **Honor the living landscape.** Caves and confluences are not props; they are persons in a continental drama, and they deserve consent.

2. **Separate romance from record.** Single-source sensations without verifiable correlates don't qualify as discoveries. The 1909 story remains a captivating newspaper feature, not an archaeological site report.

3. **Let anomalies refine you.** When cave chronologies misbehave, don't burn the data—improve the methods. Learn how water and time sculpt both rock and evidence.

4. **Keep portals in the picture.** Sacred geographies aren't superstition; they're technologies for shaping humans. The cave remains one of the world's best-designed classrooms.

Field Notes for Co-Investigators (That's us.)

If you ever retrace these stories, carry these habits:

Start with the stewards. In the Canyon, that means tribal voices first. When a Hopi cultural leader says "the confluence is our emergence," treat that as a living claim, not a metaphor to be mined.

Read policies like maps. Cave closures are not voids; they're contours that reveal what is fragile or sovereign. Translate "No Entry" into "This matters."

Trace sources to ground. If everything points to a single century-old article and nothing points to artifacts, notes, or verified locations, you are in the country of legend. Enjoy it—don't mistake it.

Stay with the questions. Anomalous cave chronologies don't dethrone whole paradigms overnight, but neither do they deserve sneers. The right posture is neither credulity nor contempt but curiosity wedded to method.

Caves of the Americas are not empty rooms. They are braided with breath, habitations of bat and springtail, classrooms for initiates, repositories of paintings and offerings, and, yes, theatres for humankind's desire to anchor wonder in stone. The Hopi still point to an emergence and live in its teachings. Park biologists seal caverns not to hoard but to protect. Tourists say "forbidden" because mystery still works. And a newspaperman once spun a city from a cliff face and lit imaginations for a century.

Our task is to keep the awe and sharpen the method. The ground deserves nothing less.

If Chapter 5 taught us to listen for flooded kingdoms, Chapter 6 teaches us to hear the ground's whisper: *down is a direction in space, but also in the self.* The caves of the Americas—sacred, sealed, storied—still open for those who approach with the right blend of awe and honesty. That is the only password they have ever required.

Part III: Myths, Monsters, and Forbidden Knowledge

Chapter 7: The Guardians of the Deep

The mouth of a cave is a promise and a threat. Step inside, and the air chills, sounds compress, and daylight folds itself into a coin you could slip into your pocket. It's in these thresholds—wells, sinkholes, tomb-shafts, cenotes, lava tubes—that the oldest stories place their sentries. Serpent's coil there. Giants lurk there. Chthonic beings—those rooted in the under-earth—watch there, at the gates between worlds. This chapter enters those gates with you, not as a preacher of certainties but as your co-investigator, treating myth as a kind of fossil that still carries the fingerprints of the people who made it, and testing it wherever possible against archaeology, ecology, psychology, and the engineering of ancient sites.

Along the way, we'll meet snakes that drink oceans, guardians that straddle species, and a royal class of subterranean intelligence called Nāgas who, in India and Cambodia, become law-givers of rivers and engineers of rainfall. We'll also ask sharper questions: Why do so many "underworld" myths put hybrid creatures—half human, half animal—on the door? What is the ancient logic of making a gatekeeper from two lives at once? And when stone circles and carved pillars speak in animals, what sort of science is hidden in that grammar?

Serpents, Giants, and Chthonic Beings: A Field Guide Across Worlds

Every culture fashions a bestiary for the thresholds. In the Hellenic world, the Python guarded Delphi's omphalos, and the Hydra stung from a swampy cusp between land and lake. Norse myth casts Jörmungandr—the Midgard Serpent—into the sea that rings the world, its bite poised to close the cosmic circle. Egypt's Apep thrashes along the nightly river of the sun; Mesoamerica raises feathered serpents to span earth and sky; Aboriginal Australia's Rainbow Serpent writes river courses the way a stylus writes a score. Across North America, horned serpents keep house in springs and sinkholes, and in East Asia, dragons are not only storm-bringers but magistrates of waters, tunnels, and fog.

Where there are caves and charnel houses, there are vultures—carved, painted, or winged in ritual costume—chaperoning souls through an aperture in the north of the sky, as though the Milky Way were a hallway and the rift in Cygnus a door. On a 12,000-year-old limestone hill in today's Türkiye, serpent reliefs swarm across pillars in early sanctuaries, while a later stone shows vultures involved with the passage of a human head—underworld custodian meets avian psychopomp, in a single panel of prehistoric theology.

Beneath these snakes and birds stands another perennial figure of the deep: the giant. Giants are mountain-sized memories—of Ice Age scale, of megalithic shock, of the time when people burrowed and bridged stone. Some giants live on in folklore as wild men—shaggy cave-dwellers seen at the edge of settled land, halfway between human and beast. Reports of such beings—call them European woodwoses, Central Asian almas, North American Sasquatch—have long sat at that friction point between ethnography and zoology. The conservative conclusion is that these figures are myths' way of personifying wilderness; a less cautious reading notes that "wildmen" traditions and sightings have been collected, weighed, and debated by scholars and naturalists for centuries—even into modern cryptozoology—precisely because threshold stories breed threshold facts.

Why the Underworld Hires Hybrids

Put your hand on a threshold—door, bridge, cave mouth—and you feel two temperatures at once. Hybrids are myths' way of making that sensation visible. A gatekeeper that is part human and part other—serpent, bird, bull, catfish—announces a boundary that is also a blend. But there are deeper mechanics at work.

First, the neuropsychological. In trance, fasting, rhythmic exhaustion, or chemical ecstasy, humans reliably see certain geometries and composite beings. Cave painters and ritual specialists across continents rendered exactly these: lattice grids, zigzags, spirals, and then—through the tunnel of patterns—therianthropes, those human-animal fusions that populate the deepest chambers of rock art. The consistency of this vision language is striking and has been studied across San rock art, Upper Paleolithic caves, and ethnographic accounts of shamans; the hybrid is not a decorative whim, but an experience report, a map glyph for a change of state.

Early Serpents of Stone

In the earliest excavated sanctuaries at Göbekli Tepe, one enclosure's pillars teem with carved snakes. Nearby, a later "Vulture Stone" panel links vultures, a severed human head, and other motifs consistent with a belief in soul-transfer and skyward passage. Early ritual landscapes are speaking the language of guardians—and they're doing it in animals.

Second, the ecological. Subterranean and liminal waters are full of partial creatures: blind fish with vestigial eyes, salamanders that look like animated roots, eels that slip between river and sea, snakes that swim better than they slither. If your livelihood depends on springs and caves—if your city's life is a karst system—you will meet these half-lights often. Hybrids become mnemonics for water safety, for the rules of entry: bring a guide, mind the gas and the silt, watch the snakes at the lip.

Third, the political and the sacred. Gatekeeping is a technology. Guilds of miners, well-diggers, and stonecutters—the earliest engineers— naturally encoded the thresholds they controlled with guardians: serpents that bind, bulls that butt, birds that escort. In a world where knowledge is ritually gated, a hybrid on the lintel is both a warning and a membership test. And when early cults experimented with altered states—whether through dancing, deprivation, or psychoactive mixtures—the guardians they met in trance returned with them as temple reliefs and doctrine. On that same limestone hill in the Fertile Crescent, coiling snakes appear in such profusion that the enclosures feel like amplified dreamscapes—visionary nets frozen into stone.

Finally, the cognitive-symbolic. Hybrids are metaphors with bones. A snake-man says, "Here, knowledge sheds skins." A vulture-woman says, "Here, we disassemble to pass." Myth adopts these creatures because language alone cannot manage the physics of thresholds.

Serpents Below, Birds Above: The Oldest Gate Signs

Pull at the snake thread and you find yourself in the oldest stone precincts. One early sanctuary's "Snake Pillar Building" concentrates serpent imagery into a mesh: bodies interlaced like a net, heads downcast as if descending. Another precinct pairs vultures with a disembodied head and a scorpion—an icon set that reads cleanly as psychopomp, soul, and southern constellation. The vultures' job in such panels is precise: to carry essence—the head as soul—out of its old address. The snake's job is equally precise: to bind, to cure, to poison, to transform. When such signs cluster around a floor of polished lime or a standing pair of monoliths with human hands carved along their sides, we are in a room that stages a passage.

Archaeology bolsters this reading with off-site echoes. In Neolithic Anatolia, vultures appear with headless figures in shrine panels that unmistakably ritualize excarnation and soul-transfer. At a proto-Neolithic site farther east, the severed wings of large raptors were cached and likely worn as costumes—humans taking bird-shape to conduct duties among the dead. Myth calls them "Guardians"; archaeology catches their feathers in the act.

And it is not incidental that serpent imagery has long accompanied medicines and intoxications. Across early ritual contexts, bowls and basins sit alongside carving programs rich in snakes—just where you'd expect paraphernalia if altered states were being engineered as part of initiation. When visionary practice and serpent iconography cohabit, the "guardian" becomes not only a monster in stone but a state of mind the initiate must meet—and survive—to pass.

Giants at the Margin

What Hybrids Do At Doors

1) *Signal a boundary worth ritual.*
2) *Encode field rules (don't descend alone; respect water).*
3) *Stage a psychological shift—"Now you are not only yourself."*
4) *Claim the door for a guild, a cult, a lineage.*
5) *Translate trance into architecture.*

Giants feel different from serpents and vultures. If snakes are chemistry and birds are ceremony, giants are geology: personifications of cliffs, erratics, and glacier-polished bones. Their haunting ground is the liminal topography—caves, boulder fields, mountain passes—where human scale is perpetually humbled.

Folklore's wildman, the woodwose, is the giant's ground-level cousin. He is the "maybe" of anthropology: a being whose reports and iconography spread across continents, yet whose bones remain elusive. Even so, the dossier is not trivial. Classic art shows hairy, club-bearing figures among mounted hunters; medieval manuscripts have dogs harrying a muscular, man-shaped beast; colonial observers in the Pacific Northwest dutifully record Indigenous fear and respect for mountain-dwelling "others." For our purposes, the wildman belongs in this chapter not as proof of a zoological species but as proof of a cultural logic: the deep place gets a deep guardian, a liminal person to match a liminal ground.

If you work mines, fell forests, and push roads through mountain throats, you invent stories that look you back in the eye and ask, "Who told you the earth was yours?" Giants do that work. Their bodies carry the ethics of excavation.

Case Study: The Nāga of India and Cambodia

No guardians of the deep are as administratively competent as the Nāgas. Where many serpents simply menace or mentor, Nāgas govern. In Sanskrit sources, they are semi-divine serpent beings dwelling in **Pātāla** (the netherworld) and in every watery interface—springs, tanks, rivers, the ocean's skin. They hoard and release rain, manage treasure, adjudicate wrongs, and teach kings. Their royal houses stack in the under-earth the way dynasties stack above, and their names— Shesha, Ananta, Vasuki—are synonyms for support and span: a serpent that upholds the world; a coil that measures cosmic time.

In India, the Nāga portfolio is broad:

- **Hydrology & Weather.** As guardians of rivers and groundwater, Nāgas are petitioned at snake-shrines for rain and for the health of tanks and stepwells. Regional cults—Bengal's Manasā, Karnataka's Nāga-bānas—tend live serpents and stone coils in groves where aquifers breathe.

- **Cosmology.** In the icon of the **Ocean Churning**, a many-headed Nāga becomes the rope with which gods and demons churn the sea to extract ambrosia. It is a technology myth: hydraulics as theology.

- **Kingship & Law.** Nāgas can withdraw waters to punish bad rule and restore them when justice returns. They are the underworld's civil service.

In Cambodia, Nāgas scaffold a civilization. The founding legend of Funan tells of an Indian voyager who marries a Nāga princess; Khmer kingship thus inherits both Vedic sky-rites and the serpent's water-rites. Walk the causeways of Angkor and you hold their bodies in your hands: **Nāga balustrades**—massive, multi-headed serpents—run along bridges to temple cities, literally forming the railings you grip as you cross moats and barays. Here is symbolism you can trip over:

- Crossing a moat into a temple framed by Nāgas dramatizes entry from mundane time into sacred time, under serpent auspices.

- The **barays** (vast reservoirs) and canal grids of Angkor are hydrological scripture: the kingdom's survival depends on monsoon capture and release. Nāgas on causeways are not decorative flourishes; they're signatures of the water-management state.

- Multi-headed Nāgas at gateways invokes multiplicity (seven or nine heads), signaling the many tributaries of the Mekong and the many mouths through which blessing can arrive.

Nāga lore also walks the seam between **under-earth** and **under-mind**. In trance and vision, serpents tend to appear first—coiling ropes, lattices of scales, snaking tunnels—before the humanoid mentors arrive. In that grammar of experience, the Nāga's mixed portfolio makes sense: part animal guide, part technologist, part judge. It also helps explain why Nāga images colonize **threshold architecture**—bridges, portals, temple gopuras, and well-heads. The visitor passes, but first, the pass is stamped.

Hybrid Logic, Tested: From Vision to Stone

When you stand before a prehistoric pillar gridded with snakes, or a carved bird escorting a tiny human head toward the north of the sky, it is tempting to hear only poetry. But the evidence for **repeatable** liminal experiences—visions that closely rhyme across cultures, especially in subterranean and ritual contexts—is strong. Detailed neuropsychological models link the ladder of geometric entoptic to the emergence of composite guides; ethnography documents the training of ritual specialists to enter, endure, and report such states; archaeology keeps returning bowls, basins, and benches to rooms where those reports are chiseled into stone. These convergences are exactly where myth stops being "mere story" and becomes a **method** for managing passages—through grief, through initiation, through dark spaces, through drought.

Back on that high Anatolian mound, serpent programs concentrate in one enclosure so heavily that scholars have read them, plausibly, as representations of visionary snakes—icones of the "active spirit" of intoxicants and medicines—and therefore as didactic devices for initiates: "This is what you will meet; this is how a body changes." On another pillar, a vulture manages a human head, while a scorpion anchors the panel to a segment of the sky. An early literature of passage, written before the alphabet, has survived in an animal.

A Cautious Note on Giants and Wildmen

As we close this circuit of guardians, a sober caution belongs here. The line between **monster as metaphor** and **monster as mammal** is not always sharp, and the literature on "wildmen" has seen its share of both romantic credulity and reflexive dismissal. What matters for our theme is that the **role** persists. Whether literal or literary, the wildman's job description is constant: hold the boundary of the deep, trouble the extractive impulse, test the trespasser's ethics, and occasionally teach.

Reading A Threshold Panel

1. *Identify the sentry. What animal form guards the seam (water-gate, cave-mouth, bridge)?*

2. *Find the human token. Head, hand, heart, infant, or shadow figure = the person part of the passage.*

3. *Check for sky hooks. Scorpions, birds, constellations: which direction of heaven does the door open to?*

4. *Track the tools. Bowls, basins, benches: clues to ceremony; look for "pharmacy" signs near snakes.*

4. *Royal contract: position a king or priest in respectful proximity to signal governance under Nāga mandate.*

Where the serpent instructs transformation and the bird escorts essence, the giant polices appetite.

Threshold of Evidence
(Interview with a Wildman)

Why These Guardians Matter Now

Thresholds are not only topographic. They're temporal and civilizational. Water tables drop; aquifers salt; heat drives animals (and people) to new doors. The old grammar of guardians is a technology we still need: **serpents** to remember that medicines are double-edged and that transformation hurts; **vultures** to remind us that endings must be escorted properly; **giants** to ask whether our dig is a theft. Nāgas, in particular, remain exemplary: they tie rulership to water ethics; they put public works—reservoirs, canals, steps—under ritual supervision; they make you cross a serpent before you enter power.

Beneath the myths, then, the unflinching lesson is practical: treat thresholds with liturgy and with data. Instrument your wells; sing at your bridges. Let your city remember that hydrology is a sacred office. If we listen, the guardians tell us exactly how to act.

The Door as Teacher

Imagine one last descent. A stepped well spirals down, its walls slick with monsoon memory. Oil lamps prickle a constellation out of the dark. On a landing, a stone serpent curls, nose toward the water; above, carved wings unfurl, carrying a tiny, round head into the north of the night. On the final step, a footprint worn a millimeter deeper than the rest says someone stood here often, breathing slowly before the plunge. That, too, is a guardian: the imprint of all the people who remembered to pause.

Chapter 8:

The Suppression of Subterranean Lore

The first time you hear the word "underworld," your mind probably reaches for myth—Anubis weighing hearts, Orpheus bargaining with shadows, heroes descending and returning with a new law or a new fire. But say "underworld" to a field ranger staring at a sinkhole, to a geologist reading a fracture map, to a speleologist scrubbing decontaminant off her boots, to a parish priest answering late-night questions about spirits and tunnels, or to a department chair passing on a student's strange thesis about "sealed caves and lost cities," and you'll notice the same reflexive move: a door quietly shuts.

We've been trained to live on the surface. This chapter pries at the latch.

I'm going to show you why institutions recoil when stories turn downward; how public-facing explanations ("safety," "conservation," "no evidence") sometimes conceal deeper anxieties about authority, narrative control, and reputational risk; what the paper trail says— policies, orders, and declassified programs that circle the subterranean; and then we will walk you into one of the most contentious terrains in North America: the closed and contested spaces beneath Mount Shasta.

The Surface Reflex: Why Governments, Churches, and Academia Reject Underground Myths

Let's start with a simple claim: modern institutions do not primarily adjudicate truth; they manage risk. Subterranean lore—tales of cavern worlds, sealed tunnels, and things that don't fit—threatens to multiply risks of several kinds at once.

Government: liability, secrecy, and the ecological veto

At the policy level, governments have very good reasons to restrict caves. The Federal Cave Resources Protection Act (FCRPA) authorizes managers to *withhold* the locations and characteristics of "significant caves," explicitly carving out exemptions from public-records release. In plain language: you can file a Freedom of Information Act request asking for sensitive cave maps, and the answer can legally be "no."

FCRPA isn't a conspiracy; it's conservation. Cave ecosystems are fragile, bat populations are collapsing in places, and a single careless visit can seed a fungus that wipes out a hibernaculum. Agencies from the National Park Service to the Bureau of Land Management have repeatedly used closure orders to protect caves, particularly since the emergence of white-nose syndrome (WNS), which led to multi-year shutdowns and permitting regimes.

This is the ecological veto: biology trumps curiosity. It also means that datasets, maps, and sometimes entire sites drop out of public view. When lore swirls around those same sites, official silence looks like suppression—because, functionally, it is. Not orchestral, not sinister; just policy that happens to sound like a locked door.

But there's more. The government's interest in underground environments runs far beyond caves as habitats. Consider DARPA's Subterranean (SubT) Challenge, a multi-year effort to build autonomous systems capable of mapping and navigating mines, tunnels, and caves—explicitly because such environments are "too dangerous, dark, or deep to risk human lives." In other words, the state funds cutting-edge exploration technologies for the exact environments that folklore says hold secrets. That doesn't prove legend; it proves attention.

And then there are safety-driven "blank spaces" on the map—temporary closure orders around wildfires, debris flows, or unstable volcanic slopes—that happen to coincide with rumoured entrances. Those orders can last months to years. Their legal language reads dry as dust; their cultural effect is rocket fuel for myth.

The Three Keys Of Official Silence

Key 1: Confidentiality by law. FCRPA allows agencies to withhold cave locations and sensitive details.

Key 2: Closure by biology. WNS-related orders shut entire cave systems to prevent human-mediated spread.

Key 3: Safety by season. Fire, rockfall, flood-risk, and unstable snow/ice fields justify rolling closures that often look arbitrary from the outside.

Churches: doctrine, discernment, and reputational firebreaks

If the state fears injuries and lawsuits, churches fear contagion of a different kind: spiritual malpractice. Subterranean lore often overlaps with the liminal—spirits in caves, initiations in darkness, underground sanctuaries. Traditional faiths are comfortable asserting metaphysical realities; they are cautious about specific *locations* where those realities allegedly break into the world. That caution becomes a reputational firebreak: better to say "no" to sensational claims—and distance yourself—than to validate a story that later unravels.

Historically, religious traditions acknowledge underworld motifs (Sheol, Hades), sacred caves, and descent narratives. But discernment frameworks treat novel, localized claims as spiritually ambiguous at best. The institutional reflex is to redirect believers toward recognized texts and liturgies—not toward field expeditions into rumor. (That redirect is pastoral—but read from the outside, it is suppression by reframing.)

Why Sacred Institutions Side-Step Cave Stories

- *Ambiguity of source: Are the experiences angelic, ancestral, psychological, or deceptive?*
- *Moral hazard: Sensational claims attract grifters; leadership protects flocks by depriving scammers of oxygen.*
- *Doctrinal sufficiency: If salvation does not require spelunking, no cave should become a sacrament.*

Academia: parsimony, peer review, and the "anomalous evidence" trap

Scholars are trained to hug the mean—to prefer explanations that require the fewest new entities. If a claim about a city beneath a volcano requires rewriting geology, archaeology, and history, it's going to face an uphill climb. That's not bias; that's the discipline of parsimony.

But the academy has another reflex that matters here: it tends to quarantine data that does not fit prevailing models. Whole careers have documented this social dynamic—the way out-of-family evidence gets minimized, deferred, or framed as error until a paradigm shift forces a re-read. The phenomenon is real enough to have a literature of its own, and in the context of deep time and human origins, it has been argued that "anomalous evidence" is often handled not by refutation but by neglect. That observation—whether you accept the authors' broader conclusions or not—is germane to subterranean lore, because it explains *why* claims about forbidden caverns rarely receive a fair audit: they arrive already *coded* as noise.

If you add to that the fact that caves are liminal research spaces—hard to access, ethically fraught (burials, living species), often encumbered by confidentiality clauses—you can see how "no evidence" can be a self-fulfilling artifact of access regimes rather than a decisive verdict on the story world itself.

FROM DISCOVERY TO DISAPPEARANCE

Lifecycle of a stray data point in scholarly publishing

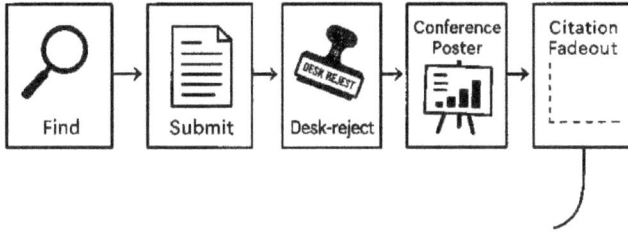

What the Paper Trail Shows: Declassified Programs and "Sealed" Areas

You asked for the documentary spine of this chapter—the dry papers that, when read with care, illuminate the shadowed corners. Here are four categories that matter.

A) Legal confidentiality of cave data

As noted, FCRPA (16 U.S.C. Chapter 63) explicitly protects the "nature and location" of significant caves by exempting them from disclosure. The statute authorizes permits, penalties, and a management program—plus the power to withhold sensitive information from public release. The result: maps, biological reports, and cultural resource notes can be real but unreachable.

The NPS operationalizes this in its cave/karst policy library: managers are instructed to close caves or portions of caves for safety or resource protection, and to restrict disclosures when necessary. If you've ever wondered why some cave descriptions exist only as carefully denatured summaries, this is why.

B) The white-nose shock and the ecological closures

White-nose syndrome altered the map. Beginning in 2006–2011, as mortality exceeded 90% in some hibernacula, agencies closed caves en masse to slow the spread. Those closures weren't whispers—they were press releases, orders, and signage—and many remain in modified form, with permit systems and strict decontamination regimes. If your grandmother hiked a lava tube in the 1980s without a permit and you can't, this is the driver.

California documented the fungus that causes WNS across multiple counties in 2024, with state wildlife authorities amplifying protocols. Nationally, BLM and the Park Service have formalized cave closures and permitting tied to WNS risk. Ecologically, this is non-negotiable; culturally, it supercharges subterranean rumor by shrinking lawful access to already rare environments.

C) Government R&D in underground environments

The SubT Challenge (2018–2021) is a clear, above-board demonstration that the U.S. Government actively pours resources into subterranean problem-solving: mapping, comms, search-and-rescue, and hazard detection. Replace "mine" with "mythic tunnel," and the toolkit is similar. This is not a wink toward lost cities; it's a sober

How Cave Confidentiality Works

- *Statute: FCRPA gives legal grounds to withhold.*
- *Regulations: Interior's 43 C.F.R. Part 37 provides the identification and management framework.*
- *Practice: Agencies publish closures and general guidance; they keep specifics in restricted files.*

recognition that the underworld—literal, constructed, or natural—is operationally consequential.

D) Rolling land closures that intersect the rumor

Browse the alerts for the Shasta-Trinity and Klamath National Forests and you'll find a living ledger of closures: wildfires, unstable slopes, post-storm hazards, and trail safety. Many are nowhere near a cave; some are. For a local who has heard a tale about a "sealed passage," a fresh forest order around that drainage becomes interpretive kindling. The language—"to provide for public safety"—is sincere but opaque, because officials don't (and often can't) explain the *precise* hazard or sensitive resource.

Why Underground Myths Persist: The Deep Grammar of Descent

We also need to understand *why* people keep telling these stories even when institutions demur. Humans have been using caves as ritual theatres since deep prehistory. Caves generate altered acoustics, absolute darkness, and sensory conditions that peel back the usual cognitive filters—no surprise they become places of encounter in every tradition that has them. Modern explorers and psychonauts have argued that these thresholds can open into visionary pedagogy—tutelary beings, codices in the dark, doorways that rewire a life trajectory. Whether you catalog these as neurotheology or as encounters with "the ancient teachers," the cave as portal is a persistent cross-cultural pattern.

Other researchers have tracked how long memories of catastrophe—floods, fires from the sky—petrify into epics about vanished lands and sunken kingdoms. In that memory-work, mountains become arks, caverns become libraries, and the survivors are imagined to have preserved arts and sciences in stone wombs during a long winter. From there to legends of "keepers" in hidden halls is a short step.

If you add to this the sociological fact that anomalies often get handled by exclusion, you have the perfect recipe for a counter-canon: a literature of the "things not allowed," curated by outsiders precisely because insiders refuse to host the debate.

The Anatomy of a Subterraneaen Legend

Threshold	Trigger	Transmission	Tension	Telos
– The Cave	An Accident or Closure	– Interpreters	– Official Silence	The Legend

Five stages in one cave's story

The Anatomy Of A Subterranean Legend

- *Threshold: A cave, mine, or lava tube with history.*
- *Trigger: An accident, a closure, or a remarkable experience.*
- *Transmission: A community of interpreters (locals, climbers, seekers).*
- *Tension: Official silence or denial.*
- *Telos: The legend ripens into teaching—moral, mystical, or conspiratorial.*

Declassified Files on Cave Expeditions and "Sealed" Areas: What We Can Say with Confidence

A caveat: the phrase "declassified files on cave expeditions" conjures Indiana Jones. Real files look like *memos*—policy, permitting, enforcement, or research programs. When agencies share details, they typically concern **how** to manage risk, not **what** was found. But the record does demonstrate the following:

1. **A lawful framework to keep secrets about caves.** The FCRPA statute and implementing rules explicitly authorize confidentiality. NPS policy documents echo this with practical management directives, including partial or complete closures. That means redactions and "no records" responses can be the result of lawful withholding, not absence.

2. **Documented, multi-year cave closures nationwide for WNS.** Reports and orders beginning around 2010 show agencies temporarily closing dozens of caves, then migrating to targeted seasonal restrictions and permitting. The scientific driver (protecting hibernating bats) is overwhelming. The cultural effect: an entire generation learned that "caves are closed," and rumors took root in the dark.

3. **Active federal investment in subterranean search/mapping tech.** DARPA's SubT literature—finals at Louisville Mega Cavern in 2021—spells out the objective. These are not secrets; they are signals that what lies underground matters strategically.

4. **Rolling closure orders in sensitive landscapes (including the Shasta region).** Safety-driven orders are public; their causes (especially where they intersect sensitive biological or cultural resources) are often not. Expect maps with big red polygons and little context.

Case Study: The Closed Zones Beneath Mount Shasta

Mount Shasta is not just a volcano; it's a mirror held up to American imagination. Ask three locals and you'll hear five stories: Native traditions of spirit beings and cosmic battles; settler-era traveler's yarns; New Age mapmaking; cryptid catalogs; UFO pilgrimage. And at the center, a durable motif: an underground city called **Telos**, peopled by the survivors of a lost continent—Lemuria—connected to the surface by a web of tunnels.

Let's ground this in the land, then read the lore against it.

How To Read A Closure Order Like A Pro

- *What's cited? Note statutes (e.g., 16 U.S.C. § 551) and regulations—these tell you whether the order is resource-protection or pure safety.*
- *What's not said? If a closure references bat maternity, archaeology, or "sensitive resources," assume confidentiality rules are in play.*
- *Is there a map? Compare the polygon with known karst/lava features on geologic layers; overlap can be suggestive.*
- *Sunset clause? Look for dates; repeated renewals hint that the underlying issue persists.*

The Ground: Volcano, lava tubes, closures

Shasta proper is a stratovolcano with complex glacial and hydrothermal systems. The **regional** subsurface is pocked with lava tubes from older basaltic events; the most famous publicly accessible tube near the mountain is **Pluto's Cave**, northeast of Weed. It's not "under Shasta" in the cinematic sense, but it is part of the wider volcanic field and a magnet for explorers. The Klamath National Forest's visitor page notes Pluto's Cave, with safe penetration limited to roughly a quarter mile for casual visitors; no permit is required, but posted rules apply.

Layer on bat stewardship and you get the pattern we've seen nationwide: educational programs, periodic access restrictions at certain caves (especially maternity or hibernation sites like nearby Barnum Cave), and a drumbeat to respect closures and decontaminate gear. California's wildlife authorities, for their part, have confirmed the WNS fungus in multiple counties and maintain reporting and response protocols; that puts managers on high alert for any cave visitation that could vector spores.

Meanwhile, in the Shasta-Trinity National Forest—the massif's south and west—public-safety closures rotate: wildfires, trail hazards, washouts, avalanche debris. They rarely mention caves because the immediate concern is often above ground. But for communities primed to expect "sealed entrances," the living map of closures looks an awful lot like confirmation.

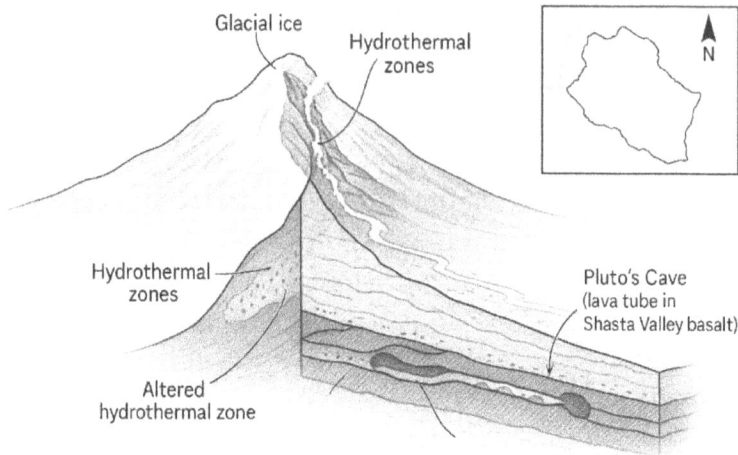

Mount Shasta–Shasta Valley Geological Section (Pluto's Cave context)

The Lore: Telos, Lemuria, and the teaching city underground

The Mount Shasta–Lemuria complex is not an internet fad; it's a century-old narrative arc that fused late-Victorian occult geography with California's frontier mysticism. The story matured through books and orders, then went pop in the twentieth century, attaching itself to

> **What We Know Vs. What We Can Test (Mount Shasta)**
>
> *Known: Pluto's Cave exists and is managed; other regional caves are real and sensitive. Safety and WNS closures are a matter of record.*
>
> *Unknown but testable: Are there significant unmapped tubes or voids within the edifice that connect to accessible entrances? (Geophysical surveys, hazard permitting, and ethics apply.)*
>
> *Not testable with current access: Claims of a fully realized subterranean city (Telos) remain in the mythic register absent verifiable entry and documentation.*

UFO culture and, more recently, to wellness and "ascension" currents. It's a myth with stamina because it offers a **why**, a just-under-the-surface intelligence stewarding human progress. That fulfills the same narrative function that older civilizations assigned to underworld watchers and teachers. (Across traditions, the "below" is not just hell; it's a library.)

Deep cave art research and modern visionary accounts, for their part, show why the setting is so persuasive: underground darkness is a known catalyst for encounters with the numinous and the pedagogical—adversaries and allies both—making it the natural architecture for a "teaching city," whether you interpret it neurologically or metaphysically.

The Friction: Closures meet cosmology

Take a living myth that promises revelation and place it on a mountain where land managers *must* close areas for fires, rockfall, and bat stewardship. Then add lawful confidentiality around cave resources. The result is inevitable: locals swap maps; visitors whisper about "gates welded shut"; a new closure order drops on the website, and a dozen narratives bloom.

Rather than mocking that human response, a better approach—and the one we adopt for this book—is to *work the seam* between policy and folklore. What follows is a concrete, ethical field method for writing the Mount Shasta chapter of subterranean lore without trespassing or contaminating the biome.

A Field Method for Ethical Inquiry at Mount Shasta

1. **Start with the paper.** Download all current Shasta-Trinity and Klamath alerts and closure orders; build a timeline for the zones mentioned in local stories. Note where closures recur seasonally (bats, snow hazards) versus episodically (fire, post-storm).

2. **Overlay geology.** Use publicly available geologic layers to identify basaltic flows and potential tube-forming units. Cross-reference rumored locations with the map; mark what falls on private, tribal, federal, or municipal land.

3. **Respect the ecological veto.** If a site overlaps bat maternity or hibernation habitats, do *not* enter, even if access seems physically possible. The ethics of WNS are non-negotiable. (Review state wildlife guidance for reporting observations; learn decontamination protocols even for legal caves.)

4. **Favor lawful access.** Pluto's Cave is open within limits and serves as an excellent training ground for reading lava-tube morphology, collapse windows, and airflow hints. Use it to sharpen your eyes so you don't go blundering into off-limits terrain.

5. **Collect oral histories as data, not dogma.** Treat every account as a *layer*: when, where, what was seen/heard/felt, and what

---

Field Gear For An Ethical Underworld Survey

- *Helmet + two independent light sources (with spare batteries)*
- *Gloves, knee protection, eye protection*
- *Mask and decon kits (follow current WNS protocols)*
- *Flagging tape (biodegradable), survey notebook, laser rangefinder*
- *Permit or printed closure orders for the area you are visiting*
- *A second person who knows when and where you're going— and when to call for help*

changed afterward (a fence, a welded gate, a new sign). Don't argue; map.

6. **Do not publish coordinates for sensitive features.** If you discover an unrecorded entrance, route your notes through appropriate channels for evaluation. The goal is to be part of the stewardship, not to burn a site.

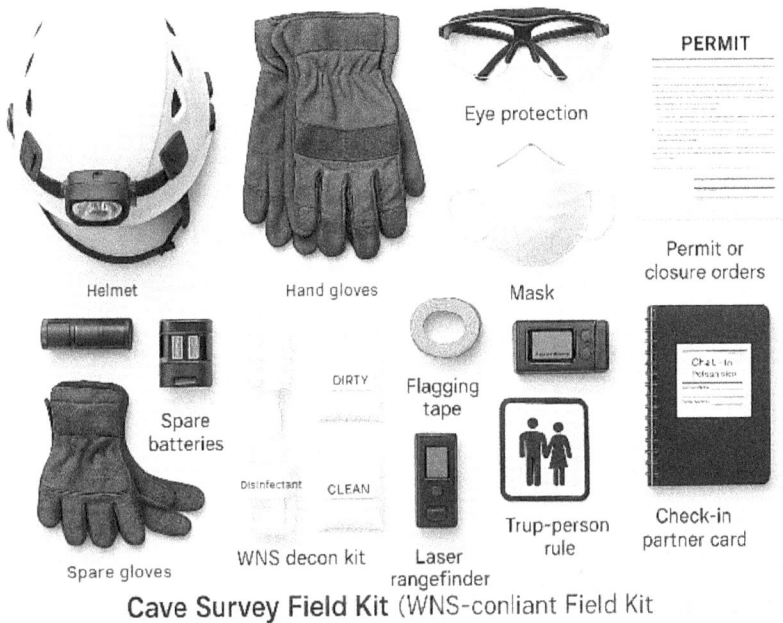

PERMIT

Eye protection

Permit or closure orders

Helmet   Hand gloves   Mask

DIRTY

Flagging tape

Spare batteries

Disinfectant CLEAN

Trup-person rule

Check-in partner card

Spare gloves   WNS decon kit   Laser rangefinder

Cave Survey Field Kit (WNS-conliant Field Kit

How We Wound Up Here: Watchers, Catastrophes, and the Memory of Stone

If Mount Shasta's Telos is a modern myth with ancient bones, it's because the underworld has always been cast as a school. Stories of "watchers," guardians, or tutelary figures in the hills and mountains are part of a long civilizational memory in which the sky and the underground are linked—north stars and soul paths above, bones and libraries below. In several strands of alternative prehistory, mountains, and caves are depicted not merely as refuges but as *laboratories* where a shattered world re-learned how to live after catastrophe. This idea—that beneath us, somewhere, lie the archives of a prior order—animates both classical "antediluvian" narratives and modern speculation about advanced knowledge sequestered in rock.

Why does the academy flinch? Because if even a fraction of those transmissions proves true, they would alter chronologies and lineages and embarrass experts. Why does the state flinch? Because refighting culture wars over metaphysics is not in any agency's mandate, and because unmanaged crowds wreck habitats and get hurt. The result is a managed silence—a suppression that is equal parts prudence and paternalism.

Writing the Case Forward: Mount Shasta Without the Noise

Let's sketch, as you might present it in your narrative voice, a sober Shasta section.

Begin with a dawn approach on the Everitt Memorial Highway, the cone throwing a long shadow, the air smelling faintly of volcanic glass warming in the sun. In the town, shelves of books about portals and Lemurians crowd next to maps of trailheads and avalanche advisories. The mountain is a palimpsest: Klamath, settler, seeker, scientist.

"Under Shasta," people tell you, "there are doors." Sometimes they mean Pluto's Cave; sometimes an unmarked gate on a service road; sometimes the memory of being led into a room in a dream. The closures on the forest website read like a slow heartbeat—open, closed, open—while the statues of angels in shop windows point down as often as up.

You carry two maps: the public one, and a second that exists only in stories. Where they overlap, proceed. Where they diverge, linger—this is where disciplines fail to talk to each other.

In a lava tube, you kneel by a cold wall, headlamp off, while the last of the light drains away. In that watchful dark, consider the arguments: geologists warn of collapse; biologists beg you to leave sleeping bats undisturbed; guardians in robes promise instruction if you can just find the right door; bureaucrats insist on protocols; skeptics tell you there is nothing here but stone and the theater of your nervous system.

Now turn the lamp back on and do the brave thing: **hold all of it**. Respect the closures, learn the biology, note the policies, record the stories, and refuse to reduce a complex mountain to a single verdict. That is not fence-sitting. That is a mature investigation.

Putting the "Suppression" in Perspective

So, is subterranean lore being suppressed? Yes, but nuance matters.

- **By law and policy, deliberately.** Agencies withhold locations and close caves for resource protection and safety; their silence around specifics is intentional and defensible. (It also feeds rumors.)

- **By culture, reflexively.** Churches and universities are conservative by design; they guard boundaries and shun sensationalism. That protects communities from charlatans and keeps methods clean—but it can also delay worthy inquiries.

- **By narrative gravity.** Humans *want* a hidden city because we want a teacher—especially one who lives where authorities won't go. That desire makes us vulnerable to both deception and revelation. The remedy is not derision; it's discernment.

If you feel that something grand and old is sleeping under mountains, you're in good company. Civilizations across time have whispered the same. Some framed those whispers as poetry; others as cartography. A few went underground and came back changed—and painted what they saw on rock.

What we can do—what this chapter has fought to do—is keep the investigation brave **and** clean. If the underworld is a library, your conduct is your library card. If the underworld is a mirror, your intent is what stares back.

We will continue, in later chapters, to test the claims that survive first contact with ethics and evidence. For now, the lesson from Shasta and the policy world is clear: the underworld isn't just hidden; it's **managed**. Knowing the managers' rules is not selling out; it's the only way to stand at the threshold without breaking what you came to understand.

The Playbook For Responsible Subterranean Inquiry

1. *Obey closures and permits. You are not above the bat.*

2. *Separate access from evidence. A locked gate is not proof of a secret; it is proof of a lock.*

3. *Document rigorously. Dates, times, coordinates (withhold in publication), source attributions.*

4. *Hold two truths: Myths teach; ecosystems break.*

Chapter 9

Caves as Gateways to Other Realities

We descend together.

Not just down a slope of damp limestone, but into a human habit older than cities and farming: the urge to go under— to slip past the crust of the everyday and cross a threshold that cultures across time have treated as literal. In the dark, breath pooling into faint clouds, footsteps softening into rhythm, the walls begin to breathe back. Overhead, a bead of water gathers, falls, and echoes like a bell struck in slow motion. The senses stretch; the ordinary world thins. Historically, that's exactly the point: caves were built (or selected) to change minds.

You and I will read this chapter as co-investigators: curious, grounded, and unsatisfied with easy answers. We'll explore why shamans, oracles, and initiates go underground to alter consciousness; how acoustics, darkness, and expectation collaborate with neuropsychology to forge "gateways"; and we'll anchor it all with a close case study—the Oracle of Delphi—whose subterranean chamber made politics pivot and empires hesitate.

The Oldest Door: Why Humans Enter Caves to Meet "Others"

Across continents and millennia, initiation tales converge on the same mise-en-scène: a mouth in the rock, a passage narrowing to a chamber, and a person tasked with returning different from how they entered. An Inuit novice walks in trance to a cliff face "where a cave-mouth, not previously visible, will open," slipping into a world that closes behind him and risks keeping him forever; Maya ritualists describe caves as the true entrances to **Xibalba**, a water-filled underworld where spirits live and the beloved dead reside; North American and South American accounts alike send would-be healers into decorated caverns to meet teachers behind the stone's thin veil.

This shared vocabulary—cave as gate, descent as ordeal, return as rebirth—helps decode the haunting Ice Age art hidden deep in European cavern systems. There, shamans trekked far from sunlight to paint hybrids and beings that look exactly like what modern practitioners and lab volunteers report in visionary states: therianthropes, lattices, vortices, cascades of points, and grids that "float" into figures. The cave, in this reading, isn't a gallery; it's a device, a medium tuned to a human neurological capacity for entering altered states and perceiving a "spirit world."

Field Clues: Is This a "Portal Cave"?

Look for: extreme remoteness from daylight; constricted squeezes into broader chambers; water-sounds or still black pools; surfaces conducive to echo; traces of lamp-soot; negative handprints and "meander" motifs; siting near springs or fault lines. These are the architectural signals of intention, not accident.

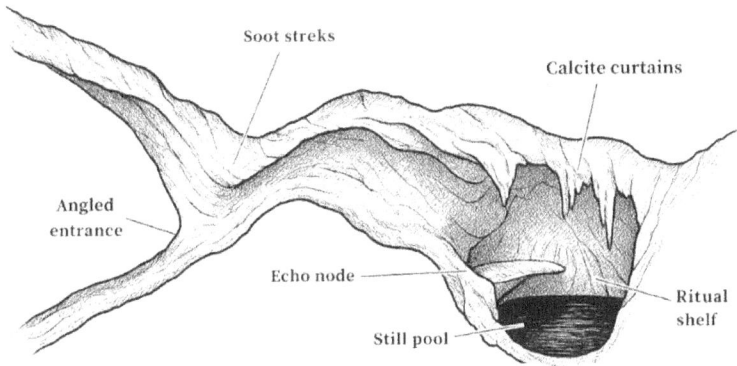

Soot streks

Calcite curtains

Angled entrance

Echo node

Still pool

Ritual shelf

ANNOTATED SECTION OF A LIMESTONE (KARST) CAVE SYSTEM

5 m

Ritual Technology: Darkness, Echo, Flicker, and the Brain

Caves are not passive settings; they sculpt perception. In near-total darkness, the brain heightens gain on the faintest inputs, spontaneously generating **entoptic** patterns—lattices, zigzags, dots, spinning webs—that many cultures interpret as the first layer of a different reality. Push deeper—through drumming, hyperventilation, dehydration, fasting, sensory restriction, or plant catalysts—and those geometries transform into **iconic** visions: animals, human-animal hybrids, presences. This three-stage phenomenology, repeatedly seen in ethnography and lab settings, neatly predicts the forms on cave walls and explains why artists crawled to the farthest rooms to make them.

Ritualists also encountered a recurring inner "architecture": a spiraling **vortex** or rotating tunnel whose sides appear patterned like stacked grids, a feeling of being pulled downward and then **through**—as if the correct destination lay beneath the floor of the world. That "tunnel" is reported so consistently in deep trance accounts that it becomes a motif; painted in caves, it is often rendered as meanders and nested grids. The walls themselves become the vortex's skin; the chamber is the throat.

Acoustics. Caves speak. A stray clap blooms into a chorus; slow chant couples with the chamber's resonance, creating beat frequencies that rise and fall. The human voice becomes bigger than a body, and the **echo** acts like an answer—a call-and-response with the stone. Paleolithic groups sought out "vast echoing chambers," not for comfort but for effect; ritual designers know that a long, warm reverb bends time and fuses voices into a single organism. With flickering lamplight—shadows shimmying across relief—figures seem to step forward from the rock itself. It is not surprising that witnesses felt beings **"floating" through a thin membrane of stone**, surrounded by scintillating geometries.

> *The Cave as a Mind-Amplifier*
>
> - *Input: Darkness + monotone sound + flicker light + scarcity + story.*
> - *Process: Entoptic → iconic transitions; soma sensations (stings, cuts, pressure) reinterpreted as "spirit surgery."*
> - *Output: Convincing encounters; symbolic death-and-rebirth; communal knowledge to bring back.*

The Initiatory Ordeal: Wounding, Dismemberment, and Return

From Siberia to Australia, from the Arctic to the Americas, initiation myths encode the same sequence: the candidate is pierced, cut open, disassembled, destroyed—then reassembled and **returns** carrying new power. The images in caves of "wounded men," speared and stocky, appear to be visualizations of this ordeal, not mere hunting mishaps. Ethnographic records echo with initiates who report being pierced with lances, their bones removed and cleaned, their organs replaced with stones or crystalline "darts," and snakes or light set into their heads— a language of **spirit surgery** applied to somatic hallucinations felt as stings, darts, or pressure. The universality of the script suggests a stable psychological choreography of becoming a healer.

Plant Catalysts and the Descent Motif

Altered states can be achieved by breath and beat, but Upper Paleolithic peoples also had access to botanicals whose effects align with the visionary art we find underground—**psilocybin**-bearing mushrooms and potent members of the Old World nightshade family among them. In such trances, the descent experience is near-universal: a pulled-down feeling, a rushing tunnel, passage through water, and then a luminous domain that feels not conjured, but **discovered**. For artists who had already trained their communities to treat caves as "concrete symbols of passage into another world," it was natural to marry plant portals to stone portals—and memorialize the journeys in pigment and incision.

When Stones Become Synthetic Caves: Twin Pillars and "Soul Holes"

Some ritual centers **build** the cave they want. At Göbekli Tepe, twin T-shaped pillars dominate elliptical enclosures whose very geometry evokes womb and **axis mundi**. Between those pillars—and through porthole-like stones—initiates may have imagined transferring consciousness into a twin "placenta soul" to move between worlds. The architecture functions like a portal: ecstatic dancing, drumming, sensory deprivation, and the ingestion or inhalation of psychotropic preparations are the "keys" that make the threshold work. In this way, open-air sanctuaries simulate the psychological effects of subterranean descent.

Ethnopharmacology 101 for the Underworld

Not a recipe—an interpretive lens. In visionary states: (1) entoptic lattices → (2) iconic beings; (3) descent/vortex; (4) binding encounters that feel "more real than real." The point is not intoxication, but information.

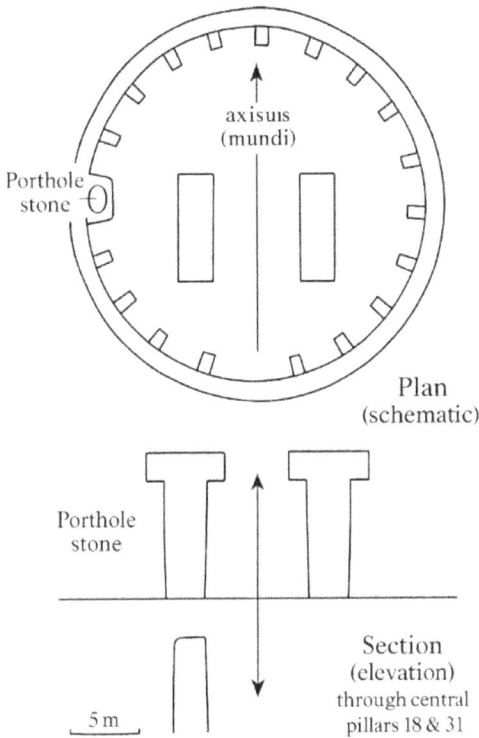

Göbekli Tepe Enclosure D:
Plan & Section (schematic)

Acoustics, Darkness, and the Neuropsychology of Cave Rituals (Deep Dive)

Let's take apart the "machine":

1) **Darkness** removes visual grounding cues. The brain fills the vacuum with internally generated patterns—the entoptic suite. When a group **expects** to meet presences, the mind's "best guess" is guided accordingly. The ritual script pre-loads the hallucination with culturally specific actors.

2) Flicker from fat-lamps or torches creates stroboscopic illusions on uneven surfaces. Paintings or engravings "move," protrusions become snouts, shoulders, wings. Each wave of brightness raises arousal; each darkness trough deepens inward focus.

3) Echo and resonance deform one's voice into something "Other." The chamber's reverb time and modal frequencies cooperate with chant to create an externalized reply. In a large, rounded room, even a whisper can sound like a choir. It's the perfect feedback loop: call, echo, confirm.

4) Story supplies the frame. "There is a crack in the wall; a man will appear in it. Do not look away." In countless accounts, that is exactly what happens: stone **splits**, and a teacher steps out.

5) The brain's thresholding completes the crossing. As laboratory and field reports show, vision often starts with **lattices and spinning grids**, then yields to fully realized beings. Many describe a **rotating tunnel** or **spiral** of squares—exactly the kind of patterns Paleolithic artists traced and dots they sprayed.

When shamans and volunteers describe contact with "freestanding realities," some investigators propose the brain as a **receiver**, not just a generator—tuned by endogenous or exogenous chemistry into channels normally opaque. Whether one accepts the receiver metaphor or not, the **family resemblance** between the motifs on cave walls and the phenomenology of trance is too tight to be accidental.

Case Study: The Oracle of Delphi and Her Subterranean Chamber

When Greeks wanted answers from the gods, they climbed to a temple built over a **navel**—an **omphalos** set at the center of the earth. The stone itself signified the axis that joins worlds, the **adyton** beneath it the space where a mortal woman—the Pythia—spoke for a power that was not her own. She did so **after breathing vapors rising from a** chasm in the rock—a detail that, even stripped of later speculation, locks Delphi into the same tradition as the cave shrines of hunters and shamans: access is **down**, via a natural breach in the ground, where gases, springs, and acoustics conspire with expectation to produce oracular speech.

Delphi's cosmology is explicit. The omphalos marks the center where Zeus's two eagles met; an invisible umbilical cord ties the sanctuary to the axis of the sky. The Pythia's descent—literal or architectural—puts her at the crossing of earth and the divine. Far from an aberration, Delphi exemplifies the **structured** use of subterranean architecture to engineer liminality: a chamber below the public eye; a restricted entrance; ritual protocols; a voice amplified by architecture and belief.

The Long Experiment

For ~25,000 years, humans used caves as controlled laboratories to test and refine states of consciousness—and then publish the results on the walls for the next generation to read. That's not superstition. That's method.

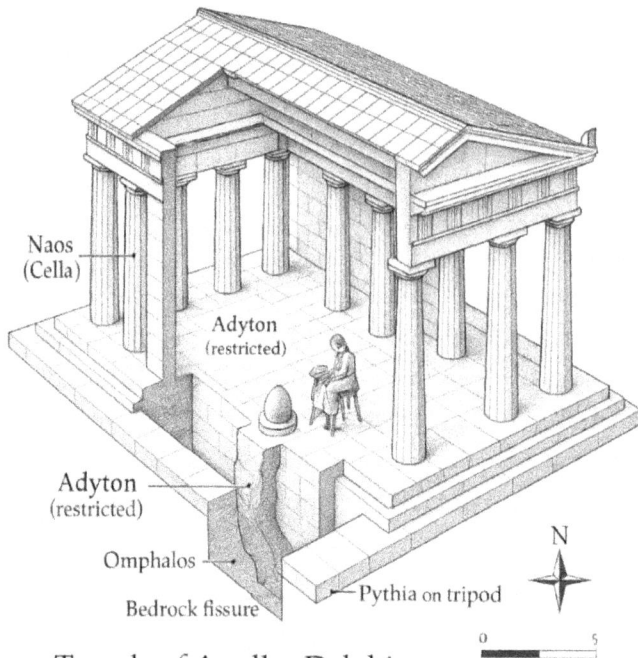

Temple of Apollo, Delphi
— Cutaway Axonometric

Delphi also clarifies a broader pattern: sanctuaries at the center of the world often **pair** a vertical axis (mountain, pillar, omphalos) with a **subterranean** breach (cave, chasm, spring). This duet tells the body what the theology asserts: the middle is where up meets down, and **that** is where speech from "elsewhere" can be heard.

Shamans, Oracles, and Initiates: Entering Altered States Underground

Put the pieces together—the descent motif, the neuropsychology, and the architecture—and the parallels sharpen.

- **Shamans** across cultures report entering caves that **close behind them**, undergoing symbolic death, learning from beings inside, and returning with techniques for healing. The cave is not only a place; it's a **process** imposed on the senses and the self.

- **Initiates** in hunting and agrarian societies undertake ordeal scripts—piercing, dismemberment, reassembly—that match both images in European caves (the "Wounded Men") and ethnographic accounts from Siberia, Australia, and the Americas. The underground setting intensifies the suffering and the subsequent claim of rebirth.

- **Oracles** formalize the same dynamic: a prepared person descends to a sanctified under space, breathes, chants, sits, and then **speaks** as a conduit. Delphi is simply the most famous instance of a Mediterranean pattern that shadows the Paleolithic one.

What the Cave Walls Are Saying

Go back to Cougnac, Pech-Merle, Chauvet; walk into the Franco-Cantabrian dark with a lamp the way an Ice Age painter did. You'll see negative handprints—ghosts of presence—then **meanders** and grids, and then beings that are not simply animals, but **becomings**—owl-men and bison-men, lion-men, dancers with antlered heads. Ethnography and modern laboratory work give us the decoder ring: entoptic → iconic transitions, somatic pain interpreted as attack or surgery, and a finale where the traveler is given a **task** to bring back. The cave is the lab book; the figures are the published result.

Practical Investigations: How to Study a "Gateway Cave" Today

A field-tested approach you can replicate as a demonstration:

1. **Light discipline test.** In a safe cavern room, set one tallow lamp (or LED set to warm flicker) behind a small rock lip so that light reaches the wall as an intermittent wash. Place a

painted (or paper) silhouette on a relief surface. Film, then view. The figure **moves**. The rock appears to breathe.

2. **Echo mapping.** Have a chanter hold a sustained tone and move around the chamber while a second person logs positions and perceived "loudness" or "fullness." You will identify resonance **nodes** where sound acquires uncanny power.

3. **Entoptic induction (safe, sober).** In darkness, ask silent observers to report first visible forms after 5 minutes, then 10. Collect descriptions. You will likely get dots, webs, and grids. When a scripted myth is introduced beforehand, the **same** geometry will be construed differently—evidence of how narrative shapes perception.

4. **Threshold choreography.** Rehearse a procession: artificial constriction (crawl), first chamber (pause), second chamber (chant), third (silence). The **sequence** changes the brain state. The architecture writes the liturgy.

Returning to Delphi—One More Time

Rotate the Greek temple in your mind's hands. The bright colonnade is a theater set; the decisive scene plays **below**. The omphalos is the stone-age idea of the **navel** updated—an axis marker set precisely where a chthonic breach gives access to a not-here. The tripod is a piece of human factors engineering; the Pythia's breath and posture are part of the recipe. What rises from the crack (whether earthy, sweet-smelling gases or the unquantifiable breath of expectation) is less important than what the architecture and script compel: an **answer** from someone else.

That is what caves do when cultures train them to: force the mind to the edge of itself, then offer it a staged, resonant way to cross.

Frequently Misread: "Superstition" vs. "Technology"

Dismiss the underground as superstition, and you miss the sophistication. These were **technologies**—repeatable, teachable, and optimizable—combining architecture, acoustics, lighting, pharmacology, choreography, and story to induce precise mental states. Over tens of thousands of years, people perfected them. A line from this long experiment runs straight through Ice Age cavern sanctuaries to Göbekli Tepe's synthetic caves and the marble steps at Delphi.

Standing at the Mouth

Picture yourself at the lip of a chamber. Dots are becoming constellations. Breath is becoming wind. Somewhere ahead, water ticks in the dark like an antique clock. Whether you read what comes next as the brain's theater or the touch of something that isn't confined to brains, the practice is the same: a descent, a meeting, and a return.

We descend together—and we come back with something to say.

Part IV: Patterns and Possibilities

Chapter 10: The Archetypal Underground Journey

The earth has always had two faces. On the surface: the bright skin of meadows, rivers, cities, and sunlit roads. Beneath: an older face—cool, echoing, veined with rivers of stone and memory. People descend into that second face when the world above stops making sense. In the torch-lit chambers of caves, in barrows and tunnels and labyrinths, in dream-shafts and the "lift doors" of trance, humans have long enacted an itinerary older than history: the underground journey.

The underground is a stage and a teacher. It unmoors our senses; it scrambles sound, dilates time, and erases the horizon line we depend on to tell what's real. This is why the descent appears everywhere—from Homeric poetry to Amazonian initiation rites, from the ballcourts of the Maya to the modern emergency room, from seasonal myths to the testimonies of people who swear they were taken "down and away" by nonhuman intelligences. Whether our guides are hooded psychopomps or chrome-skinned technicians, the plot remains weirdly consistent: a call, a crossing, a trial, a teaching, and a return—if we're lucky—with something worth the risk.

We're going to travel this itinerary together, as co-investigators. We'll place myth beside measurement, legend beside landscape, the lab report beside the shaman's song. We'll look for solid ground without losing our appetite for wonder. And we'll keep one hand on the rock—because the underworld, while fertile, is not a place to wander without a thread.

Why the Underground Pulls Us

Start with the physiology. In darkness, the visual cortex, starved of stable cues, leans harder on its internal generators—hence the zigzags, dots, grids, and serpentine lines that so often bloom behind the eyes. Caves throw back sound in ways that summon presence. Heartbeats thicken; a drop of water becomes a footfall; the hush itself becomes a voice. Underground spaces are womb-like and tomb-like at once: liminal chambers where death and birth are metaphors that trade masks. Add to this the practicalities of ritual: a place where fire speaks louder, where a song can move rock, where a whisper can be sanctified. Small wonder that so many initiations require a plunge into the earth.

Archaeology keeps turning up the same choreography. Passage chambers that force a crouch and a shuffle; narrow "soul apertures" that suggest thresholds between zones; underground rooms tuned to resonant frequencies that shake the sternum and quiet the chatter of the mind. The neutrals will call it performance architecture. The devout will call it a door. Both might be right.

Inside the Adyton

Restricted space. Chthonic crack. Vapors. A seated medium. Questions posed by elites. Answers ambiguous enough to be universal and precise enough to terrify. It's a technology of uncertainty harnessed for governance.

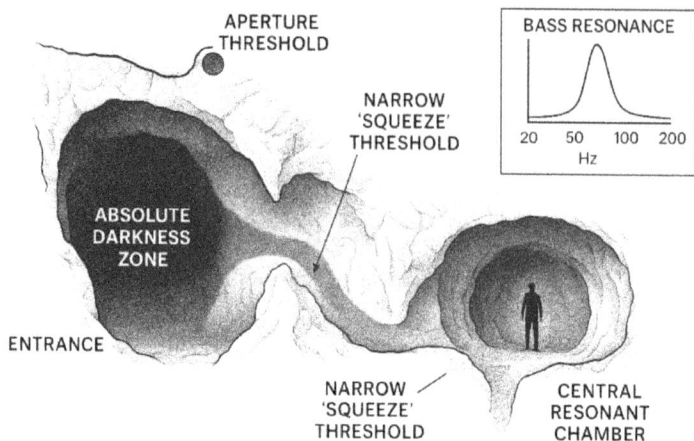

APERTURE THRESHOLD

NARROW 'SQUEEZE' THRESHOLD

BASS RESONANCE

20 50 100 200
Hz

ABSOLUTE DARKNESS ZONE

ENTRANCE

NARROW 'SQUEEZE' THRESHOLD

CENTRAL RESONANT CHAMBER

From Descent into Hades to Modern Abduction Lore

The old stories speak with different accents, but their grammar is the same. A few examples—only a sampling, because the chorus is global.

Greece and Rome: Odysseus pours black blood into a trench; the dead rise to speak. Orpheus descends for love, looks back too soon, and loses Eurydice. Aeneas walks with the Sibyl, plucks the golden bough, and returns carrying the weight of destiny. There is always a guide, always a prohibition, always a test.

Mesopotamia: The Queen of Heaven goes down. At each of seven gates, she surrenders an emblem—crown, necklace, girdle—status stripped to skin. Below, she is judged and fixed to a hook. Only through clever substitution and intercession does she return. The lesson is stark: power cannot bypass the laws of the deep.

Egypt: The night bark glides through twelve hours of darkness, past serpent chokepoints and lakes of fire. By dawn, the sun-soul is renewed. It's not simply a map of the afterlife; it's a manual for daily rebirth.

Celtic Worlds: The mound is a door. Music lures heroes into the sidhe where time loses its spine; what feels like a night is a century. Return always exacts a tax—age in a single breath, a taboo broken, a bond recalled.

Norse Lands: A god dies and is mourned across the worlds. Messengers ride to the gates of Hel, bargaining with the cold queen for a release. The terms are cosmic: if every being weeps, he returns. Inevitably, one refuses. There is always an exception, and it always matters.

The Americans: The Hero Twins accept games in a city of trials—razor ballcourts, houses of cold and jaguars, a death that is not the end. Heads are cut and transformed; life learns to grow from what is thrown away. Elsewhere, people speak of a sipapu—a little hole in the earth, a memory of emergence, a promise of return.

Africa and the Near East: Rivers to cross, bridges like sword-edges, weighing of hearts against a feather; a landscape of ethics made stone. In West Africa, thresholds are guarded by trickster-teachers; in Persian tradition, a shining bridge becomes narrow for the unjust and broad as a boulevard for the righteous.

East Asia: A land of the dead where food binds the eater, where leaving requires purification and memory's careful pruning. The rule is constant: do not eat the food of the deep if you wish to return unchanged.

Notice the constants: **a guide, a gate, a giving-up, a test, and a rule**. Notice, too, the moral inference: the underworld is not chaos; it is **lawful** in a way that refuses shortcuts. Even the gods obey.

Now hold those classics up to certain **modern testimonies**. People describe tunnels, hums, dazzling beings, examinations, symbolic surgeries, and stern prohibitions. Some lights teach, rooms without corners, and a sense that time has slipped its leash. Sometimes the setting is framed as a craft in the sky; sometimes as a facility below ground. Sometimes it's a clinical theater; sometimes it's a court. Then comes the **return**: an injunction to change habits; a sense of mission; a new fear of darkness—or an odd serenity. We can—and should— interrogate all of this with the tools of psychology and medicine: **sleep paralysis**, hypnopompic imagery, temporal lobe lability, cultural priming, and the narrative pressures of hypnosis. But explaining the **mechanism** of an experience is not the same as exhausting its **meaning**. Archetypally, the motifs line up: **a summons, a stripping, a trial, a teaching, and a release**—along with a rule broken or almost broken.

Carl Jung, Joseph Campbell, and the Collective Unconscious of the Underworld

Two twentieth-century frameworks help us think clearly without flattening the mystery.

The Bridge Between Worlds

The "tunnel of light" in modern near-death or abduction narratives and the "gate/bridge" in ancient descents perform the same narrative function: they mark the boundary between ordinary time and mythic time, and they enforce rules about memory and return.

Practical Use: When evaluating a contemporary account, map the motifs—guide, gate, stripping, test, rule. Patterns clarify interpretation.

The Jungian Map. The underground is the theater of the **Shadow**—not "badness," but the disowned, the unexamined. Descending means meeting what we've stored in the basement: fears of mortality, hunger for power, forbidden tenderness, ungrieved losses. Down there, we also meet the **Anima/Animus**—the inner other, often personified as a guide or tempter; the **Wise Old One** or **Great Mother** who offers tools and warnings; the **Trickster** whose tasks teach by embarrassment. To Jung, the descent is an episode in **individuation**: the ego loosens its tight grip, negotiates with deeper currents, and returns with an expanded center of gravity. You don't kill the dragon; you integrate it—or, failing that, you learn the cost of refusal.

The Campbell Plot. The underworld aligns with the **Belly of the Whale** and **Abyss** phases in the hero's journey. The hero enters a place of no maps, swallows the lesson ("elixir," "boon," "name"), and is reborn. Campbell's danger is over-patterning—seeing monomyth everywhere like constellations in random stars. The antidote is **specificity**. We should track not only structure but **texture**: the number of gates, the kind of rule, the shape of the trial. Patterns illuminate; details keep us honest.

A Synthesis We Can Use. The "collective unconscious" is less a library of fixed plots than a **toolbox of motifs** paired with a **human nervous system** that tends to produce certain imagery under certain conditions—darkness, fasting, rhythmic sound, isolation, pharmacology, grief. Culture tunes the vocabulary; biology supplies the verbs.

Case Study: Mythic Parallels Across Continents

Let's get specific and comparative. Here are three focused parallels where details shine.

The Seven Things You Must Surrender

In one lineage, the traveler to the deep passes **seven** thresholds and yields an item at each gate—regalia, ornaments, protective layers—entering naked into the law of below. In another, a maiden eats forbidden seeds and is bound to spend part of each year under the earth, tuning the seasons. Elsewhere, lovers or kings descend and face a non-negotiable rule: do not look back, do not speak first, do not eat. The lesson repeats: **no one crosses without cost.**

What binds these tales is **ritual economics.** The deep is not a place you can bribe; it demands symbolic equivalence. Stripping is not humiliation but **metabolism.** You return not because you are powerful, but because you **paid correctly.**

Practical lens: When a modern witness reports being required to remove clothing, jewelry, or personal items by nonhuman beings; when they're told not to look, not to speak, not to taste—read it through this ancient lens. These are **threshold rules** that articulate the seriousness of the space and the fragility of the return.

Games with Death: The Trial House Motif

In one Mesoamerican epic, the challengers must spend a night in "Houses" of jaguars, knives, cold, and darkness. They navigate trickster judges; they learn the rules of a lethal game; they lose their heads and learn to sing with new throats. In the Mediterranean, a youth threads a labyrinth to face a beast that is half memory, half hunger. In East Asia and the Middle East, bridges test balance; in the Arctic, shamans are cut to bones and rebuilt with iron sinews. The pattern: **ordeal transforms, but only if you consent.**

Now compare a certain kind of modern testimony: a "room without corners," beings who insist on **games or tests**—can you move this object? Can you bear this light? Can you keep your eyes still? There is often a trickster edge: answers that answer nothing, humor that pricks pride, riddles that erase themselves. Health professionals will note the overlap with dissociative states and high arousal. Mythographers will see the Trial House.

What we can test: The specificity of the **rooms**. Do underground-coded experiences produce a higher incidence of tests framed as "games" than sky-coded ones framed as "missions"? If so, that's a cultural-biological fingerprint worth tracing.

The Bridge, the Scale, and the Feather

Judgment scenes are among the most durable: a heart weighed, a bridge crossed, a monster waiting for those who overreached. In different geographies—the Nile valley, the Iranian plateau, the Himalayan foothills—the imagery shifts, but the logic holds: **measure your life against a standard, then cross if you can.** This isn't medieval fearmongering; it's a psychological technology. Knowing we must answer below helps us live **above** with attention. Modern people who "go down" and return often report a life audit with bruising specificity: not a tally of infractions, but a **felt** re-seeing of moments when they failed to do the good they knew. Some come back with lighter habits. Some come back frightened. A few come back free.

Caveat: We must resist easy flattening. A feather is not a spreadsheet; a bridge is not a bureaucratic checkpoint. These scenes are **images**, not policies. Their value lies in their power to order an inner court.

Holes in the Earth, Holes in the Heart

Across the American Southwest, small circular openings in ritual chambers mark where people say they **emerged** from previous worlds. In Atlantic Europe, stone tombs contain little round portals—some big enough for a hand, some scarcely larger than a coin—aligned with light in winter's depths. In the Caucasus and the Levant, ancient tombs and dolmens carry apertures that feel like metaphors made of stone: **a passage for breath, a passage for soul.** Walk into modern narratives and you'll hear it again: a "hatch" in the floor, a "trapdoor," a "round window" that leads to elsewhere. The symbol is an instruction: **you were born once; you can be born again.** But every birth is a kind of death.

Balanced Lens: Evidence Without Cynicism, Wonder Without Gullibility

We don't need to choose between scoffing and swallowing. A balanced method can hold the torch.

Archaeological Anchor Points.

— Subterranean complexes and hypogea with acoustically striking chambers.

— Passage monuments aligned to light at calendrical edges, suggesting ritual crossings between worlds.

— Carved apertures and symbolic thresholds that indicate a belief in **transit** rather than stasis after death.

— Rock art with layered entoptic patterns alongside animals and beings in hybrid forms—consistent with altered-state phenomenology deep underground.

Psychological/Physiological Mechanisms.

— Darkness + isolation raise suggestibility and imagery production; time sense distorts.

— Rhythmic sound and low-frequency resonance change autonomic tone; fear and calm can oscillate rapidly.

— Near-death states produce tunnels, beings, and audits with high cross-cultural overlap.

— Certain plants and breath/fasting practices reliably induce beings, geometry, and "teacher" encounters.

Cultural Scripting.

— Local myths influence **interpretation** without fully determining **content**. A person steeped in starships will frame the gate as a hatch; a person steeped in barrows will frame it as a door of stone. The **function** is alike.

Standards of Care.

— We listen carefully, map motifs, check for medical explanations, and still allow **meaning** to speak.

— We ask what **changes** afterward: addictions dropped, griefs reconciled, ethics tightened, art made. Transformation is data.

The Descent as a Technology of Change

The underground journey isn't just a story; it's a **protocol**. It trains perception and alters behavior. In traditional contexts, it's anchored by **rituals** that manage risk: fasting rules, guardian songs, prohibitions, and shared meaning. In modern unscripted contexts, people fall through the floor with no safety net—during a health crisis, a panic attack, an unplanned pharmacological plunge, or a random midnight moment when reality opens a seam. Either way, the curriculum is similar: **face what is feared, give up what encumbers, receive what is offered, and pay what is due.**

If we strip away the supernatural claims, the training still has teeth. The descent is a machine for **moral recall** and **creative reset**. If we accept the supernatural claims, the descent is also a **classroom** shared with intelligences not yet accounted for in our current models. Either way, it works.

What Archaeology Can and Can't Prove

Stones can show what people built and sometimes when; they can hint at how it felt (acoustics, light). They cannot adjudicate who or what was met in the dark.

A modest proposal for researchers:

1. Build a **motif inventory** across ancient and modern descendants.

2. Track **post-experience outcomes** (health, creativity, ethics) over time.

3. Map **place-effects**: caves, barrows, basements, MRI tubes, humming substations—do certain environments reproducibly trigger specific images?

4. Test **acoustics** and **light** as controlled variables in ritualized, ethical studies.

5. Keep two logs: **what happened** and **what it did**.

Threading Myth and Modernity: A Walkthrough

Let's stage a composite descent to see how the pieces click.

The Call. It rarely starts politely. A dream with a mouth in the floor. A diagnosis. A song that unlocks old grief. In myth: a dead loved one calling from below; a god demanding a visit. In modernity: a hum in the night, a pressure behind the eyes, a light that isn't a light.

The Guide. A psychopomp arrives—wolf, vulture, serpent, old woman, luminous child, technician, ancestor. They speak in paradox or protocol. "Do not look back." "Breathe like this." "Take the thread." "Lie still."

The Gate. A door in a mound. A hatch in the floor. A tunnel of light. The rule is stated. Payment is taken—ornaments, names, blood. The air changes. Your fear finds its voice, and you keep walking.

The Trial. The rooms: cold, jaguars, knives; or sterile light, hums, probing questions. You are asked to sing, to remember, to be still, to hold your gaze steady, to answer for moments you'd rather forget. Sometimes you fail; sometimes you are helped. The point isn't perfection; it's **alignment**.

The Gift. A name, a feather, a code, a vision of how your life knots and can be unknotted. A sense of the pattern behind the weather of your days. A thing to carry back, sometimes literal (a plant, a technique), sometimes invisible (a vow).

The Return. Rules on ascent are strict: don't look back, don't eat the food, don't break silence. Almost everyone breaks something. So the return is partial, seasonal, and costed. You go back above with a debt—service, honesty, art, attention.

After. The test isn't whether it "really happened" but whether you **live differently**. You keep a promise. You stop drinking. You call your estranged brother. You learn a song for others to use when it's their turn to go down.

MONOMYTH SIX

| Call | Guide | Trial | Gift | Return |

From Patterns to Possibilities

Our title promises both. The **patterns** are the repeating motifs and psychologies we can observe, compare, and, with care, measure. The **possibilities** are what remain open—perhaps deliberately so.

Possibility one: **The underworld is a cognitive space**—a predictable suite of experiences generated when human nervous systems enter certain environmental and ritual conditions. In this reading, truth is measured by transformation. If the descent helps us become more whole, it's doing honest work.

Possibility two: **There is also someone else there.** Not necessarily "aliens" in the pop-cultural sense—though some witnesses will insist on exactly that—but **nonhuman intelligences** that share mindspace or landscape with us, traditionally named ancestors, gods, guardians, teachers. If so, the underground journey is an interface technology—a way of **meeting** under terms that keep both sides safe.

Possibility three: **The world is layered.** The "below" and "above" are not only directions but **modes**. We're amphibians—moving between measurable daylight and meaningful night. To be fully human is to keep both maps in play without confusing them.

Practical Toolkit for Investigating Underground Narratives

Because our goal is not only to be moved but to be **useful**, here's a streamlined field method you can apply to sites, stories, and science.

1. **Site Walk:** Note entrance geometry, light behavior across the year, acoustics (clap test), airway drafts, microclimates, and any apertures/"spirit holes." Sketch the path in plan and section.

2. **Sound Test:** Hum, drum, chant at low volume. Track what frequencies bloom. Does the space "choose" certain notes?

3. **Story Map:** For any narrative—ancient or modern—tag the five elements (Guide/Gate/Gift/Grief/Grain). Note any taboos, numbers (3, 7, 12 recur), and payment logic.

4. **Physiology Log:** Darkness time, temperature, breathing rate, any pareidolic images, the moment the gut flips from fear to focus.

5. **Outcome Tracker:** Months later, what stuck? What changed? What new art, habit, or kindness was born?

6. **Ethics:** Never push others into descent. The underground is a **consent-only** space. Always have a thread: a guide, a time limit, a plan for return.

A Final Descent, For Now

Stand at the mouth. There's the daylight world with its invoices, its calendars, its warm bread, and petty wars. Behind you, people you love are laughing in a kitchen. Ahead, cool air sighs from the stone's throat. You feel the old anxiety—sharp and precise, like the moment before a truth you've postponed. You touch the wall. You step through.

Safety First

Real caves and tombs are dangerous. Never explore without qualified local guides, proper equipment, and permits. Ritual exploration can be conducted ethically in controlled environments (dark rooms, sound chambers) that model underground conditions without physical risk.

Inside, sound changes. Your heart becomes a drum. Shapes appear that are not shapes and teach what only shapes can teach. A figure waits—animal, ancestor, star-skinned physician, masked priesthood of your own better self. You surrender something at the first gate: your certainty, perhaps, or your timeline. You remember that you have always been mortal and that this is not a punishment but a curriculum. You accept a task you can explain only in a song. At the bottom, you are given something you cannot yet carry. The climb out will teach you how to carry it.

When you return—because you must return—your face will look the same to those who stayed above. But your eyes will hold a different kind of weather. You will make one repair you've been avoiding. You will listen when the world speaks in a quieter voice. You will understand that every threshold on the surface—doorways, borders, birthdays, vows—is a little underworld, a little school.

And the next time you hear a hum in the night, or a call from a mound, or a hallway that seems to lengthen as you walk, you will remember: the deep is **lawful**, the rules are simple, and the cost is always worth the gift—if you pay with attention, courage, and care.

Chapter 11

Science Meets Myth

The door into the earth rarely opens with a bang. More often it sighs—cool air breathing from a fissure, a rock giving under a boot, a darkness that has waited a million years for a curious human to lift a lamp. Step through with me. We're going to treat caves not as props for fantasy, but as engines of geology, theaters of survival, and archives of story. In these buried realms, science and myth don't cancel each other out; they rhyme. If we listen sharply, we can hear the rhyme scheme under everything: in the chemistry of dripping stone, in the way a folktale bends around a remembered shelter, in the genome's hushed record of a people who once squeezed through history's narrowest corridors and came out the other side.

I won't ask you to "believe" anything. I'll ask you to look. To ask what would have to be true—geologically, archaeologically, genetically—for a legend of subterranean worlds to hold a kernel of real experience. And then we'll test it. That's our pact in this chapter: awe tethered to evidence, curiosity yoked to craft.

Geological explanations for vast cave systems

Let's start under our feet. The planet is astonishingly good at making hollow spaces, and it accomplishes this without magic. Three broad mechanisms—dissolution, fire (lava), and fracture—sculpt most of the world's great underground networks. Each leaves a distinct signature, the way a mason's chisel leaves telltale marks in a stone lintel.

1) Dissolution (Karst):

Limestone, dolomite, and other carbonate rocks are calcium-rich sediments, many of them formed in shallow ancient seas. They look solid, but their fate is to surrender to weak acids. Rainwater absorbs carbon dioxide from soil and air, becoming a diluted carbonic acid solution. Over immense periods, that acid seeps into fractures, eats along bedding planes, and gnaws pinholes into galleries, galleries into rooms, rooms into labyrinths. When groundwater sits below the water table, the rock dissolves under phreatic conditions (rounded tubes, smooth walls); when rivers drain and air invades, vadose canyons cut down like knife strokes. The long marriage of these phases produces mazes—think of Kentucky's Mammoth Cave, where paleo-rivers and fluctuating water levels etched stacked levels like floors in a subterranean skyscraper.

As voids drain, dripstone begins—calcite precipitates from saturated water, laying down stalactites from the ceiling, stalagmites from the floor, and curtains, columns, and flowstone across walls and slopes. Each drop is a ledger entry. Uranium-thorium dating of speleothems lets us read that ledger: you can reconstruct paleoclimates, storm regimes, even the slowdown and revival of monsoons by the bands in cave carbonates, as if a stalagmite were a stalwart tree ring rooted in stone.

2) Lava Tubes:

Where basaltic lava pours like hot syrup, the surface can cool and crust while liquid fire still races beneath, then drains away, leaving cylindrical tunnels—lava tubes—often with skylights where the roof later

Karst In A Nutshell: Limestone + CO_2-rich water → carbonic acid → dissolves rock along cracks → tubes (phreatic) and trenches (vadose) → drainage lowers → cave air arrives → dripstone and flowstone grow → speleothems become climate archives.

collapsed. From Hawai'i and Iceland to the Galápagos, these tubes can run for kilometers. Their walls show flow lines and "lavacicles," and their floors preserve ropy textures that look like congealed waves. Some tubes interlink into networks; others host rare ecosystems sealed from light and weather, making them modern analogs for the kinds of lava refuges early peoples could have used when basaltic fields were the only solid ground for miles.

3) Fracture and Sea Caves (and the wild cousins):

Where waves gnaw at cliffs, they exploit weaknesses and joints, punching sea caves that boom with surf. Inland, landslides and boulder piles can form talus caves—irregular, low spaces between giant blocks. Less common but deeply important are **hypogene caves**, born from rising fluids—acidic waters charged with hydrogen sulfide or CO_2 ascending from deeper strata. These can carve giant chambers without any surface river ever having passed through, producing "phantom rivers" of corrosion: sulfuric acid forms when H_2S meets oxygen in cave air, aggressively dissolving limestone and leaving ghostly white gypsum flowers. When you see spongework walls and popcorn-like corrosion remnants high above any flood level, you're probably standing in a hypogene void, a cave made from the bottom up.

Now, if rocks make rooms, geology also sets the stage for **entrances**, and entrances shape human encounters. Pit mouths funnel cool air that exhales on hot afternoons; collapsed sinkholes (dolines) create sudden green basins—natural courtyards—where light reaches deep and water lingers. Cenotes—water-filled karst windows—form a turquoise constellation on Yucatán's limestone; their rims and cave-rivers became both arteries and sanctuaries for ancient Maya. In other words, geology doesn't just make space; it engineers the **ways** humans find, use, and mythologize that space.

> ### The Four Major Cave Styles To Remember:
>
> *Karst (dissolution), Lava Tubes (volcanic drainpipes), Sea/Talus (mechanical erosion and collapse), Hypogene (deep-sourced acids rising).*

Myths as distorted memories of real subterranean refuges

Push back hard on an oral tradition, and sometimes it pushes back with dates. Picture a village on the cusp of catastrophe—winter sharpened into a weapon, ash falling from a distant volcano, invaders cresting a ridge, or a plague wind coursing down the valley. Where do you go? If there is a cave nearby, you go into the earth. The world squeezes; the ceiling presses on your lungs; time changes shape. The days are long, voices lower, and in the dim drip, you inventory your words very carefully. When you emerge—if you emerge—you will carry out a story.

Thousands of years later, that story may talk of otherworlds and underworlds; of cities beneath and catacombs where ancestors whisper; of gods who live down there and messengers who move through vents. We misrecognize that as pure fancy at our peril. The frame of myth is elastic, but it often wraps around a core of experience: shelter beneath ground.

Let's trace a few of these memory-cores.

Underworld descents as survival scripts: Many cultures tell of a hero or a people who descend (a katabasis), confront trial, and return changed. Change the names, and you have an evacuation protocol. You have instructions for not going mad in a dark place. In cold regions, caves held constant temperatures above the killing winds of glacial winters; in drylands, they stored precious humidity and pooled water— sometimes the only liquid for days. Myth remembers both: as the realm of the dead (cold, still, echoing) and the womb of rebirth (moist, enclosing, life-giving). The symbolism isn't academic; it's observational—what breath feels like when the world above is a blade.

The building is underground:

Natural caves were just the beginning. When rock was right—soft tuffs or well-bedded limestones—humans **enlarged** what geology offered. Subterranean cities honeycomb volcanic plateaus, vast enough to harbor entire communities and their animals, complete with rolling-stone doors, air shafts, and chapels. Their primary purpose was pragmatic: evade raids, avoid taxation, ride out sieges. But live underground long enough, and the everyday starts to look ceremonial: the hall becomes a nave; the cistern, a sacred pool; the entrance, a threshold between worlds.

Why so many spirits in caves?

Because we met our dead there. We placed bones in chambers whose darkness felt appropriate to endings. We watched water percolate through stone and thought, rightly, of **time**. And here's a humbling thought from science: cave air and stalagmite growth mark long **beats** of climate. People who visited the same cave for generations would learn those beats: when the drip slows, the hills are drying; when it hammers, the monsoon is back. Myth loads those signals with meaning: the underworld grieves or rejoices.

Cave acoustics and fear:

A scrape becomes a whisper; a drip, a footstep; a bat's wing, a lash of something not of this world. In the dark, senses multiply and betray.

How Myths Preserve Memory:

Compress experience into symbol → repeat at key rites → attach to place → transmit across generations → the symbol outlives its literal referent but still points to practical knowledge (refuge, water, season).

Ancestral fears make for sticky stories. Yet those same acoustics can warn of danger: quickened percolation often precedes flood pulses; distant rumbles reveal unstable chambers. The monster is traumatized with a job: to keep children from playing too near the pit.

The seed vaults of the past:

Some of the most haunting myths speak of **vats, chambers, granaries** underground, stocked for a calamity that never fully arrived—or that did, but we do not remember its date. That is not science fiction. Anytime a community faces periodic terror—war bands, marauders, drought, dust storms—they cache food, seeds, and tools underfoot. The "treasure of the underworld" is good logistics; the dragon is your neighbor with a claim you'd rather he forget.

What Counts As A Bottleneck?

A dramatic reduction in effective population size → stronger genetic drift → loss of alleles → long haplotypes in the genome → later growth imprints a distinctive "hockey-stick" site frequency spectrum. It's not proof of caves. It's proof of survival through scarcity.

Case Study: Genetic traces of ancient bottleneck survivors

Genetics is where the planet whispers at the level of nucleotides. We can overinterpret those whispers, so let's keep our feet on the rock. A **bottleneck** is not a mythic cataclysm; it's a technical term for a time when a population's effective size shrinks so hard that chance dominates, rare variants vanish, and lineages thread forward through very few surviving lines. If a group endured months in a cave or years in a hidden valley while others perished or dispersed, we would expect **genetic signatures** in later descendants: reduced diversity in certain markers, telltale combinations of mitochondrial lineages, and patterns of linkage disequilibrium that say "there were not many of us for a while."

We'll focus this case study on one of the most compelling episodes of human prehistory: a small population that endured on the lip of a changing world and then poured out across continents—the **Beringian standstill**—and on a parallel logic in the Old World—**refugia** during glacial maxima—where subterranean shelters could have amplified odds of survival.

The Beringian Standstill: a narrow bridge, a long pause

Picture the late Ice Age. Sea levels are lower; a broad landmass, **Beringia**, bridges Siberia and Alaska, not as a thin gangplank but as a grass-steppe the size of a subcontinent. To the south, massive ice sheets wall off entry to the Americas; to the west, familiar lands; above, cold, dry winds. At some point before the great melt, a small founding population—ancestral to most Indigenous peoples of the Americas—settled in or near Beringia and **stayed**. Genetic models tell us this was not a quick crossing; it was a **standstill** that lasted long enough to let a distinct genomic profile cohere. Then the climate loosened its grip.

Coastal corridors or ice-free passes opened. The descendants of that standstill people spread in an astonishing time across two continents.

What does this have to do with caves? Beringia wasn't a cavernous land in the limestone sense. But the logic of refuge holds: the people who survived the standstill found sheltered microhabitats—river bluffs, dune-sheltered basins, the leeward sides of low hills, frost-warmed ground around springs and seeps, and, yes, in places where volcanic tubes, frost-heave voids, or large rock overhangs offered **wind-breaks** and **seasonal storage**. Where permafrost kept the soil frozen, the most dependable spots would often have been the rare places where **geothermal** warmth or **bedrock openings** made winter life sane. Those who innovated in shelter and caching—who "read" the ground for its safe pockets—handed on both their genes and their shelter strategies.

Genetically, the standstill left signals in uniparental markers (mitochondrial haplogroups like **A, B, C, D, and X** in different proportions) and in autosomal DNA that indicates a **founder effect** followed by rapid demographic expansion. Think of it as a single chord struck long ago that still reverberates in modern genomes.

Old World refugia and the cave advantage

On the other side of the world, the **Last Glacial Maximum (LGM)** pressed Europe, North Africa, and western Asia into a mosaic of harsh zones and survivable pockets. Populations retreated into **refugia**—the Iberian peninsula, the Italian peninsula, the Balkans, the Caucasus margins, the Levant—where a mix of coastlines, river valleys, and karstic hills gave them room to breathe. The genetics of later Europeans bear that stamp: after the ice eased, people expanded out of these refugia, mixing repeatedly with newcomers.

In karst lands especially, caves are not bit players. They are **thermostats** (cool in summer, less cold in winter), **water loggers** (springs and cisterns), **food lockers** (steady humidity slows spoilage), **signal posts** (you can see the valley floor from a cave mouth and retreat if danger rises), and **archives** (soot on ceilings, ash in hearths, bones in crevices). If you wanted to push a small group through a bad century, you would choose a limestone hill laced with voids, a defensible entrance, and a second exit only your kin know. You would call that place by a name that later generations would mistake for metaphor: the **Womb of Stone**, the **Mouth of Night**, the **House of First Mothers**.

The genome does not highlight caves with neon ink. But it does highlight **smallness** and **duration**. When we see lineages that show signs of extended low effective size and then sudden growth, and when those lineages coincide with regions dense in caves and rock shelters, we have a well-founded hypothesis: the people who endured there probably used the underground advantage. That is where myth's underworld and science's refugium shake hands.

A reconciliation: science's map, myth's torch

At first glance, scientific maps and mythic torches seem to light different rooms. But they can walk together, particularly underground, where detail matters and exaggeration thrives in the dark.

Science gifts, myth gifts:

Science gives us a **grammar** of stone and time: dissolution rates, flow regimes, isotope geochemistry, and the mathematics of drift. Myth gives us a **memory architecture** optimized to carry survival rules across generations: "When fire falls from the sky, go down"; "When the river disappears, follow it into the hill"; "There is a second door, but only the old woman knows which stone to push." The two are not enemies. They are halves of what a prudent species keeps in its head.

Why mainstream narratives shrug at buried worlds:

Academic habit prefers what's easy to date and widely represented. Caves bias the record. They collect flash-flood debris, preserve what would rot aboveground, and host repeated occupations that blur into each other. They can confuse us: a single chamber might hold Early Neolithic burials, Bronze Age offerings, and medieval smoke, all within arm's reach. It's safer, narratively, to treat caves as marginal—which is precisely how you write **out** of history the places where small groups likely survived the worst years. Myths refuse that erasure. They keep saying, with tireless eccentricity, "Look down."

Reading A Bottleneck In Dna—Plainly:

*Long identical segments across many individuals (IBD) →
suggests recent common ancestry from few founders. Excess of
intermediate-frequency variants → suggests growth after
contraction. Combine with archaeology (dates for hearths in caves,
changes in toolkits) and climate proxies (speleothem isotope shifts)
to time survival episodes.*

A methodology you can use:

1. **Map the stone.** Identify karst belts, volcanic fields with known tubes, and hypogene provinces.

2. **Plot the tales.** Note where underworld myths cluster, especially those with nuts-and-bolts details (doors, corridors, stores).

3. **Overlay population genetics.** Flag regions with evidence of ancient bottlenecks and later expansions.

4. **Ground-truth with archaeology.** Date hearths, soot, soot micromorphology, and speleothem surfaces; look for curated caches.

5. **Ask conservative questions.** Not "Did a lost subterranean nation exist?" but "Would sustained refuge use here materially raise survival odds?" That's a testable proposition.

Global Overlay: Karst Landscapes,
Underworld Myths, and Genetic Bottlenecks (Conceptual)

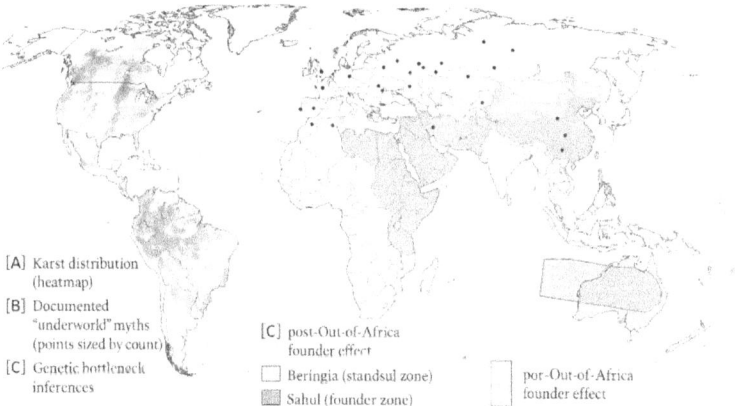

[A] Karst distribution
(heatmap)
[B] Documented
"underworld" myths
(points sized by count)
[C] Genetic bottleneck
inferences

[C] post-Out-of-Africa
founder effect
Beringia (standsul zone)
Sahul (founder zone)

por-Out-of-Africa
founder effect

How caves become libraries of climate and crisis

We cannot leave the geochemistry in the hallway. Speleothems—stalagmites and stalactites—are **books**. In their calcite are oxygen and carbon isotopes that swing with rainfall and temperature; embedded dust that whispers of wind regimes; trace elements that track vegetation shifts. If a community's story says "we went below when the world grew fanged," go to the caves. Date their dripstone growth bands. Did growth **pause**—a sign of drying—around the purported time? Do soot layers thicken then? Do hearths proliferate deeper in?

Even the cave's **skin** speaks: a patina of smoke on walls can be laser-sampled along micro-transacts to date pulses of burning. If a myth speaks of "Winter of Three Flames," and a cave's soot record shows three tight pulses of intense indoor fire around a particular interval, you have not "proved" the tale; you have calibrated it. Suddenly, the myth's cadence is less distant from the climate curve.

Living with darkness: the psychology that myths encode

Speleothem 101 For Story-Hunters:

- *Oxygen isotopes ($\delta^{18}O$): proxy for rainfall source and amount.*
- *Carbon isotopes ($\delta^{13}C$): proxy for vegetation and soil respiration above.*
- *Trace metals (Mg/Ca, Sr/Ca): hint at water residence time and prior calcite precipitation.*
- *Uranium-thorium dating: routine precision to a few decades in the Holocene.*

When dripstone growth slows or stops, something big changed aboveground.

Science handles rock well; myth handles **fear**. A group in a cave during a crisis navigates monotony caused by panic. Darkness strips away the theater of everyday social roles; new hierarchies emerge around skills that matter underground: who can find water by smell, who can read the draft, who can tell a story that steadies children when the roof creaks.

This is why so many underworld traditions begin not with conquest but with **negotiation**: "We asked permission." Even as metaphors, those lines train behavior—move gently, keep flame low, don't insult the stone. Translate the ritual into fieldcraft, and it becomes: conserve oxygen, preserve fuel, avoid ceiling spall by not pounding where the rock rings hollow. If the humans who obeyed the "spirit rules" lived more often than those who didn't, the rules stuck. They turned into gods with preferences. Those gods, in turn, became the **guardians** of caches, cisterns, and entrances.

Mythic motifs as micro-manuals

Let's decode a few recurring motifs as if they were marginal notes in a subterranean field manual:

- **The two exits:** A common underworld motif. Practical gloss: Every safe refuge has an escape route. If an entrance floods or an enemy finds it, a second, narrower chimney brings you to the slope behind the hill.

- **The river that flows backward:** Underground streams can reverse direction seasonally or during flood pulses; they "back up," turning clear pools opaque with silt. Myth marks that oddity to warn: "the water can betray you."

- **The guardian animal:** Bats, snakes, bears, wolves. Not random. Bats map airflow and seasonality; snakes mark warmth and prey; bears mark deep shelter used not just by humans. The "guardian" tells you who else uses the place and when you may not want to share.

- **The forbidden name:** Names anchor entrances. If your safety hinges on secrecy, conceal the locus with a taboo. To outsiders, it reads as superstition. To insiders, it is non-disclosure.

When legends name whole underground worlds

The grand claims—the continent-spanning tunnel systems, the entire civilizations below, the lightless gardens—shouldn't be dismissed outright, nor swallowed whole. Read them as **exaggerations of scale** built on repeated local truths. If you stitched together the mapped caves of a single karst plateau, added the lava tubes of an adjacent volcanic field, and connected them with the cultural routes that skip from one refuge to the next, you would indeed get something that feels like a **networked world below.** Messages can travel that way faster than over exposed ridges; goods can be cached station by station; whole armies can be evaded. The legend is the **regional memory** of a **logistics spine** that looks subterranean because its **critical nodes** are underground—even if the links between are above.

In the same spirit, the stories of **sunless gardens** point to real biological phenomena: troglobitic creatures (white, eyeless fish and insects) and chemoautotrophic ecosystems in sulfur caves that grow without sunlight. To people eking out a famine year, discovering edible fungi and blind fish in a hidden pool would feel exactly like finding **food that refuses the sky**. The story makes that miracle portable—teach it once, remember it forever.

Stone Shelter: Seasonal Routine

1. Entrance with rolled stone

2. Smoke test with feather in draft

3. Carving a tally of water collection

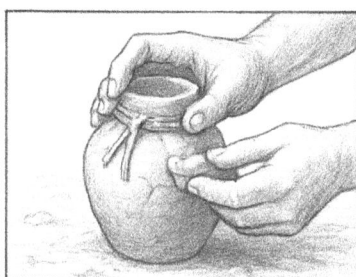

4. Sealing a seed jar with clay

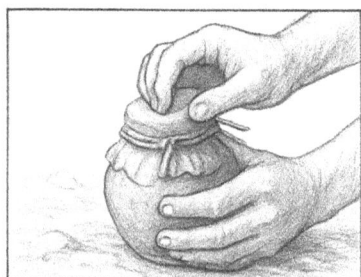

5. Spring flood sluicing the dawn

6. Family emerging at dawn

Bringing the three strands together

We promised to braid geology, memory, and genes. Here's the weave:

1. **Stone gives shelter and archives.** Caves form predictably where water and rock conspire; they preserve what the surface erases.

2. **People use stone to survive.** In bad centuries, communities retreat into voids, enlarge them, and ritualize the rules that keep them safe. Those rules ossify as myth and rite.

3. **Small groups leave narrow threads in DNA.** Bottlenecks and refugia etch their results into genomes; later booms carry those threads far. If the refugium was cave-rich, then caves were almost certainly part of the survival toolkit—even if the DNA can't spell C-A-V-E.

When mainstream history shrugs at underworlds, it's often because the evidence is uneven—caves hoard it in pockets, then hide it. But the method above lets you triangulate: rock logic, story logic, and genetic logic. If all three point to refuge, you don't need a lost kingdom to write a true, contoured history of **people who lived because they went down.**

Chapter 12

Why the Buried Realms Matter

You and I are about to walk into the dark together.

Not the darkness of ignorance, but the creative dark—the hush beneath the earth where memory keeps a different calendar. In that quiet, myths are not bedtime stories; they are survival manuals written in metaphor, routed through dreams, carved into stone, and cached in caverns for those who come after. When a culture needs to remember what it dared not say aloud, it buries the truth—in tunnels, in undercrofts, in rites enacted behind sealed doors, and in the spell-work of narrative.

This chapter makes the case for why those buried realms matter, not as props for sensationalism, but as pattern engines: places where human imagination bootstrapped itself, where catastrophic memories were compressed into legend, and where the physical ground still may conceal archives capable of rewriting prehistory. We will speak with awe, but also with clean hands and clear methods. You're not a spectator here; you're a co-investigator. Pack your field notebook. We're going in.

The Inner Map: How Hidden Worlds Shape the Human Imagination

Imagine the earliest flicker of firelight against limestone. Painted hooves surge along the wall; a ladder of dots climbs toward a crack in the rock. We tend to see "cave art" as art. But underground, art was never only art. The subterranean chamber—with its reverberant acoustics, narrow access, demanding darkness—was a tool for altering consciousness, for rehearsing cosmology, and for social memory. Caves entrain us. They compress our senses and dilate our time. They make us listen to stone.

Across cultures, underground places anchor origin stories and afterlife routes: the Duat of ancient Egypt opening in the west, the Greek Hades beneath a fissure guarded by rivers with telling names, the Mesoamerican Xibalba with its trials and "houses," the Celtic Annwn reached through mounds and lakes, the Mesopotamian Kur behind gates no sunbeam touches, the Indic Patala tiered like a vertical city of serpents. These are not interchangeable. Yet they rhyme. Each locates spiritual traffic below the feet. Each treats descent as instruction.

When a motif shows up globally despite differences in language and flora and sky, we should ask why. One answer is obvious: caves are everywhere. But that physical ubiquity doesn't explain the specific behaviors encoded—ritual descent, ordeals in total darkness, initiations staged as symbolic deaths, rebirth through a narrow "womb" tunnel, guidance by animal spirit-figures, and an emphasis on sound (chant, drum, whistle) to "open" a gate. Underground, the brain meets its theater. Stranger still: the stories remember.

What the Underworld Actually Teaches

- *Descent as a learning technology: the body is stressed (dark, cold, silence), the imagination compensates, and symbolic thinking intensifies.*
- *Memory palaces carved in rock: chambers, side-passages, and painted signs function as waypoints in a ritual narrative.*
- *Ethics of survival: myths staged below ground encode "codes" (sharing, taboo, watchword, timing) that help groups coordinate under stress.*

THRESHOLD OF THE PAINTED CAVE

Pattern 1: Descent as Social Glue

A people who descend together bind together. The underground creates controlled risk. Move single-file; mind the ceiling; don't step off the lip. Those admonitions are practical—and moral. Groups that practiced formal descents trained obedience that wasn't passive; it was cooperative. The guide learns to read anxiety. The novice learns to trust the guide. The elder remembers the inflections of the stone and passes them down: "Left hand to the wall; when it slicks, duck; when the echo tightens, you're near the chamber."

If you want to find the oldest "books" of a culture, look for the places where it rehearsed itself. Often, those places are underfoot.

Pattern 2: The Underworld as Cosmic Console

Buried spaces also serve as instruments for tuning sky to stone. Enclosures aligning to solstices; shafts aimed at particular stars; chambers that "ring" at certain frequencies—a choreography of earth, sound, and season. Faith and measurement are not enemies here; they're roommates. If people used a chamber as a seasonal clock, that ritual synchronized their planting, their migrations, and their risk management. You don't steer a community by telling them "today the declination crosses X degrees." You stage a descent that culminates in a light blade chancing on a mark, and you give that mark a story. The story travels further than the math. The math keeps the story honest.

Pattern 3: Catastrophe Memory in Disguise

Floods, fires from the sky, long winters, and "years without a summer" rarely leave intact libraries. They do leave stories. The details that survive are strikingly technical once you translate them from poetry: tails glowing in the night, stones falling that burn where they land, a darkness lasting "three sowings," rivers reversing, the sea crossing its boundary.

> ### Translating Catastrophe Metaphors
>
> - *Serpent/dragon = winding thing with power; may encode river, celestial band, or atmospheric phenomenon.*
> - *Vulture/eagle = psychopomp (soul guide) and high flier; may encode sky-watching, death rites, or star asterisms.*
> - *Twin pillars = two seasons, two gates, two limiting stars; often mark a passage between cycles.*

A great civilization does not need to tunnel under a mountain to be a "buried realm." It can bury itself in a mound, a backfilled temple, a field of standing stones re-earthed to protect or to close a chapter. And sometimes the burying is less literal: survivors inter their experience in recurring motifs—serpents that are rivers, serpents that are comets, birds that carry souls (and calendars), twins that are doorways, foxes that are trickster-signs of cycles broken and restored. Read myth like code: each animal, each number, each direction, each tool stands in for a bundle of observational detail.

SKY RIFT AND THE RIVER-SERPENT

The Ground Truth: Are There Still Archives, Artifacts, and Even Civilizations Underground?

Let's switch from what myth makes possible to what geology preserves.

The underground is not a uniform environment. It's a patchwork of microclimates and materials, each with its own rules of preservation. Dry caves (especially in limestone), volcanic lava tubes, salt domes, rock shelters beneath overhangs, abandoned cisterns, mine galleries, perennially frozen sediments, desert dunes that migrate and then lock, mudbrick acropolises that slump into layer-cakes: all of these can be time capsules. Add human intention—deliberate backfilling of a ceremonial precinct, entombment of caches beneath floors, sealing of tunnels after last rites—and you get context. Context is everything.

What Survives Down There?

- **Organics in select conditions.** Papyrus, leather, basketry, wood, and textiles can survive millennia if the humidity is low and stable, or if they're salted, frozen, or otherwise "pickled." So can pollen, hair, and residues that tell what people ate and brewed.

- **Metals and alloys.** Copper-based artifacts survive but corrode; iron often disappears unless it's in anaerobic or arid environments. Sometimes, only a rust ghost and associated soil chemistry remain. That's still data.

- **Stone, ceramic, and glass.** These are the reliable witnesses. Potsherds, beads, tools, figurines, foundation offerings, sealings, and the architecture itself—stairs, lintels, pillars, drains—are our long-lived grammar.

- **Biology.** Bat guano stratifies like a ledger; mollusk shells record water chemistry; microfauna bones date occupation; human remains, when ethically recoverable, can yield ancient DNA and isotopes that map mobility and diet.

Now scale up. Entire **subterranean cities**—not just simple cave complexes—dot volcanic and soft tuff landscapes. Multi-level chambers with ventilation shafts, rolling-stone doors, food storage, wells, stables, and chapels speak to periods of refuge, trade, and planned concealment. In other places, sacred centers rest on laced networks: drainage tunnels, ritual entrances, and service corridors no tourist ever sees. Under major mounds and pyramids, investigators have detected voids and hidden passages. In karst landscapes, sinkholes lead into cathedral-sized spaces where human hands have left marks since the last ice's retreat.

None of this requires us to imagine fantasy kingdoms thriving forever beneath the crust. But it does require us to accept that **important stores of culture**—our missing chapters—may remain sealed. Some were hidden to protect them; others were entombed by disaster or deliberate closure when a rite was retired. The deeper claim of this book is not that every legend maps to a fossilized city, but that enough do to change the baseline of our story.

PRESERVATION MICRO-ENVIRONMENTS

Benchmark: archaeoologically documented contexts

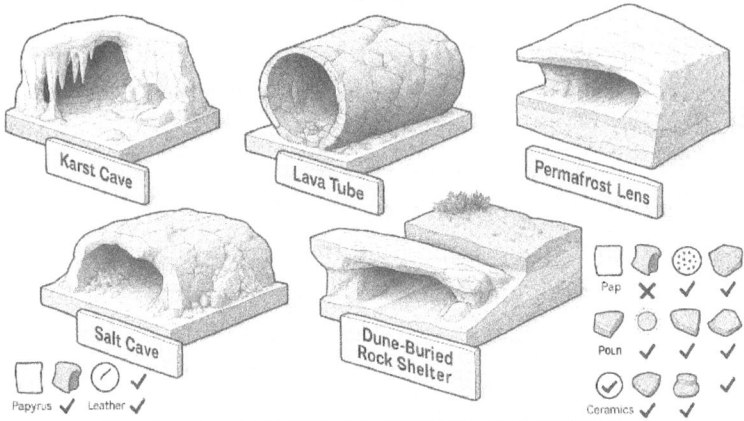

Ratings reflect consensus from archaeology; e.g., Dead Sea Scrolls (desert caves/papyrus), Halistatt
salt mines (leather/textiles), permafrost (Yukon, Siberia) preserving organics; karst cave sediments for pollen, lavas tubes.

Twelve Places Most Likely to Hide a Cache

1) Sealed karst chambers behind collapse cones
2) Lava tubes on the flanks of extinct volcanoes
3) Desert rock shelters with talus seals
4) Buried river terraces cut off by avulsions
5) Sub-floor voids beneath temples and granaries
6) Backfilled ceremonial enclosures
7) Abandoned aqueduct galleries
8) Salt caves with stable temperatures
9) Permafrost "yedoma" bluffs
10) Bog margins where anaerobic layers preserve organics
11) Cliff alcoves masked by later scree
12) Mine adits repurposed as shrines

Could There Still Be "Lost Civilizations" Below Ground?

Let's define terms carefully. A **civilization** is not only monumental architecture. It is a system with urban or proto-urban density, specialization, exchange networks, symbolic systems (writing, proto-writing, or formal icon sets), and durable institutions. If by "lost civilization" we mean a globally connected techno-utopia, that bar is high, and evidence would be loud. If we mean **regional polities and knowledge systems** that achieved surprising sophistication before, during, or outside the timelines we were taught, then yes, the underground remains the most reasonable place to find their fingerprints.

What would those fingerprints look like?

- **Anomalously early or sophisticated planning** is evident in excavated foundations: drained courts, orthogonal street grids, and deliberately infilled sanctuaries that "reset" a site.

- **Hidden knowledge architectures**: caches of standardized tokens, seals, tablets, knotted cords, or tally sticks; wall programs with repeating symbol sequences; repetitive hand signs carved on portals; "sight lines" intentionally buried with the structure.

- **Complex storage economies**: clusters of silos or jars with chemical signatures of fermented beverages, resins, oils, and dyes; residue maps that show nonlocal products held in quantity.

- **Engineering in the dark**: ventilation shafts, smoke-draw chimneys, water management tunnels crossing different strata with grade control.

- **Ritual standardization**: replicated underground layouts across distant sites, suggesting a canon—an encoded "book" of how to build and how to behave.

Methods: How We'd Find These Things

The romance of subterranean worlds is a liability unless we earn it with rigor. Fortunately, we have tools.

- **Ground-Penetrating Radar (GPR)** and **electrical resistivity tomography (ERT)** map subsurface anomalies; paired surveys help separate geology from architecture.

- **Seismic microtremor** and **muon radiography** (cosmic-ray muon tomography) can detect voids in large masses (e.g., mounds, pyramids) without intrusion.

- **Magnetometry** reveals fired features (kilns, hearths) and ditches; **gradiometry** picks up small shifts indicating walls, pits, or backfilled shafts.

- **Drone-based photogrammetry** and **LiDAR** strip vegetation and reconstruct surface micro-relief; think of LiDAR as the map that shows you where to point the instruments that see underground.

- **Geoarchaeology**—reading sediments, springlines, and paleo-channels—tells you where people could dig and why they would.

- **Residue and isotopic chemistry** turn soot, wine stone, and bone collagen into narratives of seasonality, trade, and identity.

- **Digital epigraphy** and **reflectance transformation imaging (RTI)** coax faint carvings and painted signs from rock; underground, many "blank" walls are not blank.

The Imagination's Evidence: Myths as Encoded History

A culture's "software" is myth. The underground is where much of that software was compiled. The question is not whether myths are facts in a journalistic sense but whether they are **faithful carriers of structured information.** In this book, we've followed serpents that look like rivers but also like comets; birds that ferry souls but also mark constellations; twins that guard gates but also cue seasonal switches. Let's formalize a decoding protocol and then apply it.

A Protocol for Reading Buried Myths Without Getting Buried in Them

1. **Motif Triangulation.** Take a symbol (serpent, vulture, fox, twin pillars). Collect its appearances across time and regions. Clarify the functions attached to it (guardian, devourer, guide, trickster, measure).

A Citizen-Scholar's Toolkit

You don't need a million-dollar grant to contribute:

1. *Learn to map with your phone (photogrammetry) and export to GIS.*
2. *Interview elders for place-names that mean "gate," "hole," "well," "devil," "church of the rock," or "city of ants." Toponyms are treasure maps.*
3. *Walk the edges—literally—of fields after rain and of escarpments after freeze-thaw; fresh slumps disclose old things.*
4. *Record but don't remove. Context matters more than the object.*
5. *Partner with local historians, cavers, and land custodians. Respect is methodology.*

2. **Material Cross-Check.** Ask what physical realities match those functions (river dynamics, sky features, animal behavior, seasonal cycles, astronomical events).

3. **Architectural Echo.** Look for the motif carved, painted, or encoded into built spaces and especially into underground or sealed contexts.

4. **Temporal Anchor.** Seek events (flood layers, fire horizons, climate flips) that correlate with the motif's high-energy use in texts and rites.

5. **Feedback-Loop Test.** Does the decoded reading tell you **where** to look next? If it doesn't generate testable predictions (a light effect, a buried feature, a cache), rework the reading.

Case Window A: The Bird That Opens the Gate

Across Old World and New, a large bird—often a vulture or eagle—appears in funerary and initiatory contexts. It is psychopomp and sentinel. In walled programs underground, this bird tends to occupy liminal positions: thresholds, apertures, corners where sound changes. As a sky creature, it doubles as a constellation marker; in some regions, its seasonal position highlights a passage window (migrations,

Your Notebook Rubric for Myth Decoding

- *Motif:*
- *Functions attached:*
- *Natural analogs:*
- *Built echoes found at:*
- *Dateable correlates:*
- *Prediction this reading makes:*
- *How we can test it non-destructively:*

monsoon onset, harvest). The "bird stone" motif becomes an appointment maker. When the bird "stands" in the right place in the sky, people descend.

Decoded, this is not fairy talk. It is a calendar disguised as a guardian myth. The consequence is practical: if we find an underground chamber with a bird motif at a particular sightline, we can predict the date when a beam or star hits that spot. If we're right, the chamber flickers alive on schedule; if we're wrong, the bird is mere decoration and the reading fails. Either way, the myth gives us a test.

Case Window B: Twin Pillars and the Door Between Years

Twins fraternize with pillars: two uprights and a lintel; two gatekeepers and a crossing; two seasons bound by a hinge. Underground, twin supports often frame a portal or a focal stone. In myth, twins quarrel, wrestle, die and return, trade places, or found cities at different horizons. The math in this theater can be plain: the twin uprights are a measurement casing—you can stand between them and read the sky along the lintel, or watch a blade of light complete a circuit.

Again, **testability is the charm.** If twin pillars stand in a sealed chamber with a peculiar orientation, you can model the sky for the date ranges when that orientation "meant" something. A motif becomes a time capsule with coordinates.

Case Window C: The Fox and the Broken Clock

Trickster figures—fox, coyote, jackal—mangle schedules. They steal fire, cut cords, flip seasons, make hunters miss, or swap masks at the gate. Narratively, they explain noise in the system: precession nudging last year's alignment out of true, a drought warping a calendar, post-catastrophe dislocations that demand a new cycle count. Tricksters force recalibration. Underground, fox marks placed on belts, lintels, or small figurines often appear at **reset moments** in a site's stratigraphy:

layers change, a floor is raised, a ritual set is retired, or an enclosure is deliberately buried. The fox doesn't just grin at us; it **warns** us that the clock was adjusted.

From a research view, when you see the trickster, ask what changed. Then look for the material correlate: a sudden shift in building fill, a new suite of artifacts, a different sourcing of stone or pigment, a revised icon grammar. Myth is telling you: we survived a wobble.

Why Buried Realms Matter to the Future (Not Only the Past)

This isn't nostalgia. It's navigation. We live in a century when the climate is moving fast, seas are rising, and the atmosphere is doing tricks our grandparents never saw. The ancients did not have satellites, but they had patience, pattern hunger, and the discipline of ritual observation. They tied that observation to underground architectures that forced community attention. A chamber you must descend into to see the year turn is a social clock. A narrative that makes the year's hinge a matter of collective survival is a governance tool.

Risk Manuals Hidden in Stories

When myths tell of "nine nights of wind" or "two winters without summer" or "the stone that burns the skin," they are passing down hazard memory. It would be irresponsible to go hunting single-cause explanations for every phrase; equally irresponsible to ignore the operational core of those phrases. We can extract practical counsel:

- Build where stone does not liquefy.

- Store grain where water can't reach quickly.

- Keep rituals that check the calendar even after the gadget works.

- Teach children the names of the gates, the rivers, the winds, the stars—so that when your instruments die, they can still steer by sky and stone.

Ethics: The First Gatekeeper

To dig is to take responsibility for someone else's time capsule. The buried realm is often sacred, sometimes still in active use. "Finding" is not winning. The job is careful consent, slow work, full publication, and cultural return. In many places, the most important discovery is a renewed relationship with living custodians whose oral maps are richer than any instrument's output.

- **Consent first.** If the community says "no," that is data.

- **Minimal intrusion.** Non-destructive survey before any spade hits soil.

- **Context over trophy.** A single figurine without its layer relationships is a lost paragraph.

- **Publication as restitution.** Share findings locally, in the language that matters.

- **Reburial when asked.** Closure can be part of the work.

A Field Guide to Looking Again

Let's pull your learning into a practical grid so you can apply it in the next site you meet—in person or on a page.

1) Start With Names

Place-names are stubborn. Any cluster of names meaning "gate," "well," "devil," "womb," "city of stone," "whispering hill," or "holy undercroft" merits time. Rivers that "vanish" and "return" (losing streams) advertise caves. Hills called "the watch," "the twins," or "the vulture" hint at sky ties. Names that no one can translate are often the oldest; ask three elders for their versions, and listen for the common core.

2) Read the Land's Geometry

Dry valleys with inexplicable rounded bottoms; ridges with unnatural symmetry; sudden sinks in otherwise steady fields; gullies with standing water in the dry season—these are flags. If the geometry looks purposeful, it often is. Lightly-packed backfill slumps differently than native soil; the shape of a hill can hide a stair.

3) Listen (No, Really)

Underground, your ears are instruments: a wall that "rings," a floor that "booms," a ceiling that "whispers." Old builders tuned chambers.

Five Rules for Reading Myths as Risk Guides

- *Treat numbers as ratios or orders of magnitude, not literal counts.*
- *If a story repeats a direction (west, north), assume it is a vector, not decor.*
- *If a creature repeats (serpent, vulture, fox), separate its functions: measure, guide, reset.*
- *Corroborate with sediments and tree rings before you theorize.*
- *Look for actionable lines—verbs that tell you what the community did.*

Even without a spectrometer, you can map these zones. Sound is not woo; it's a non-destructive probe.

4) Follow the Animals

Wild goats take the same impossible traverse year after year to reach salt and shelter; swallows nest at the same fissures; bats refuse dead caves. Learn their paths. The absence of bats in a "perfect" cave sometimes means the cave is too disturbed to matter—or that it is too sealed to enter easily. Both facts matter.

5) Bring the Sky Underground

Overlay star paths on site plans. Ask if the chamber you face could ever have admitted a shaft of light or framed a star. The answer is often "no"—and that's a result. But when the answer is yes, you've found a story machine.

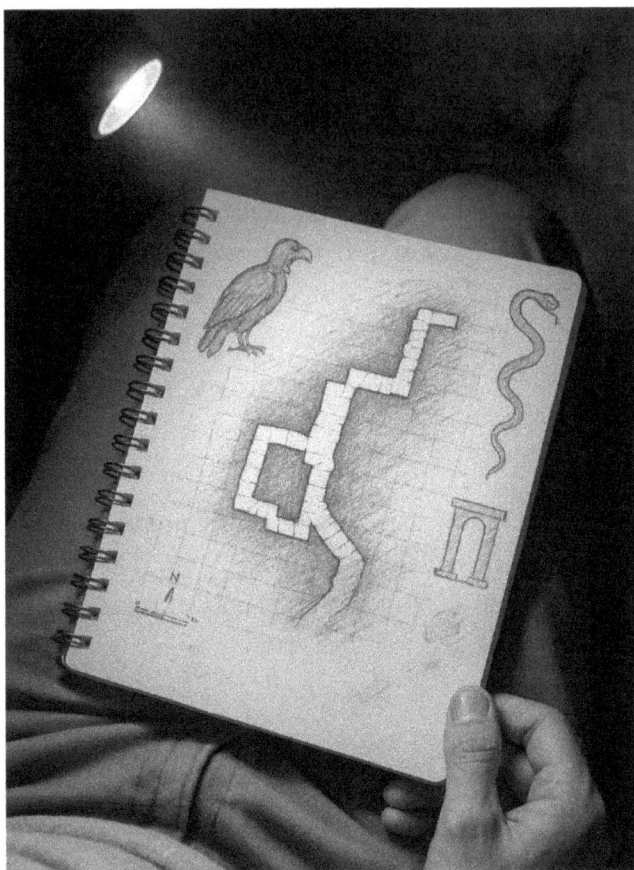

FIELD NOTES UNDERGROUND

Rereading "Fantasy" as Encoded History

This is the chapter's fulcrum: we are not asked to choose between science and story. We are asked to read a story scientifically—without squeezing it until the poetry dies, and without letting its beauty excuse us from testing.

Consider three persistent subterranean themes across world lore:

1. **A sealed place of first things**—a garden, a library, a workshop—later lost or submerged.

2. **A catastrophe that forces descent**—flood, fire, sky stone, long night.

3. **A ritual technology of return**—passwords, alignments, guides, gates, twins.

Seen together, these themes describe a cycle: knowledge stored in ritual

- *The underground is not an escapist setting; it is a problem-solving lab.*
- *Myths are not lies; they are compressed data with encryption (metaphor).*
- *We do not need proof of a global hidden empire to make this matter. We need proof—already abundant—that people used caves, tunnels, and sealed chambers to carry crucial knowledge across bad centuries.*

space; disaster stressing systems; communities using descent to keep time and keep faith; encoded memory waiting under seal until hunger returns. That is not fantasy. That's a governance model.

The Possibility Space: Archives Still Waiting

Let's get very specific about the kinds of finds that could be made tomorrow and would be decisive.

A) Standardized Symbol Sequences Underground

A repeating sequence of carved signs across distant sealed contexts that correlates with seasonal or stellar cycles would demonstrate a formalized information system. It need not be alphabetic to count as "writing." If those sequences appear alongside measuring marks (tally strokes, dot clusters) and alignment features (sighting slits, floor lines), we have a **protocol**, not mere decoration.

Prediction to Test: Where a chamber with a sign set [A-B-C] aligns to a specific date, another chamber 200 km away with the same sequence will align to the same or complementary date. If we can show this at scale, we are reading a calendar canon.

B) Deliberately Buried "Libraries"

Not parchment alone—think modular **object libraries**: standardized sets of tokens, bone tallies, carved "teaching stones," or bead strings with code positions. We already know that portable counting systems predate many scripts; a cache of such sets in a sealed underground context tied to a ritual school would prove deliberate transmission.

Prediction to Test: Where we find teaching stones in one chamber, look beneath the floor for a buried box of "faulty" or retired pieces— teaching sets often include wrong examples used to train novices what **not** to do.

C) Engineering Beyond "Need"

A vaulted underground space with acoustic tuning beyond mere practicality—nodes placed at integer ratios, resonant frequencies mapping to chants or drum patterns—would indicate **knowledge pursued for its own sake** and psychoacoustic effect. This is not decoration; it is an experimental theater.

Prediction to Test: A chamber with an "odd" small alcove at one end will reinforce a specific frequency; the associated ritual instruments (drums, flutes) found on site will match that range.

A Call: Re-Examine Myths Not as Fantasy, But as Encoded History

You and I aren't obliged to believe everything the storytellers said. We are obliged to respect the **work** those stories did. Myths are time-release capsules; they maintain a society's orientation through shock. If we read them as **encoded history**, we give ourselves another instrument for seeing through the next shock.

What does that look like on the ground?

- When we meet a tale of a sunken land, we do not chase a single island with a single catastrophe date; we map where the sea rose when, where the river moved, where silt buried a port, where salt intruded a field, where a sandbar became a graveyard of boats. The "land" sinks in chapters. The "deluge" is plural.

- When we meet a rite of underground passage as "rebirth," we read for the **skills** it trains (navigation in dark, breath control, silence discipline, emotional regulation) and the **information** it encodes (seasonal knowledge, star courses, water sources).

- When we meet a symbol animal, we ask how the **real** animal behaves—what season it arrives, what winds it rides, what calls it makes in caves—and we align that to the built space and the calendar.

A skeptic's first duty is not to say no; it is to test well. A believer's first duty is not to say yes; it is to care for the thing tested. Our first duty, you and I, is to keep curiosity warm and method cold. That is how buried realms become teachers instead of traps.

The Chapter's Core Thesis in One Breath

Buried realms matter because they are where cultures stored their best pattern recognition—about sky, water, hazard, and cooperation—inside architectures and stories designed to outlive them. If we relearn how to read those patterns, we recover not fantasies but instructions.

Walking Out of the Dark (Together)

We started by stepping into a torchlit room and letting our eyes learn the dark. We end by stepping out at dawn, blinking at a horizon our ancestors knew by heart. Between those two thresholds, the underground did a humbling thing to us: it slowed us down. It made us listen to the drip and echo and our breath. It reminded us that the things that last are not loud. They are careful.

If there are still archives under hills, we will find them because we behave as if we deserve to—patiently, ethically, skeptically, imaginatively. If there are not, the search will still have been worth it, because in the very act of looking we rehearse an older discipline: we learn to see linked systems, to hear small rhythms, to read metaphor as map, and to carry knowledge communally.

Let's leave with a simple pledge:

- We will treat myths as **serious hypotheses** about what people noticed when noticing could save them.

- We will treat underground places as **partners**, not prizes.

- We will move toward the extraordinary only by way of the ordinary work that the extraordinary requires.

The world we want—a culture that reads the signs without fear or cynicism—begins with a hand on a cold wall, a breath held before the narrow passage, and a question asked without appetite for a foregone answer.

You're ready. Pack your light. Lace your boots. Let's go find where the old stories touch the ground.

What we bury is what we fear to lose; what we dig is what we refuse to forget. The realms below are not just where the dead go. They're where the living learn how to begin again.

Bonus Section: Buried Realms Workbook

Welcome to the hands-on part of the expedition—the place where awe meets method and your curiosity becomes data. Think of this Workbook as a field journal you can use: a guided atlas of subterranean legends, a suite of reflection prompts that sharpen your intuition, a research checklist that keeps your compass honest, and a resource library that points you toward reliable wells of knowledge without draining the wonder out of the journey. We will keep both lamps lit: the lamp of wonder and the lamp of method.

Posture for every page: Mystery is not an excuse to be sloppy; rigor is not a license to be dull. Pair "Could this be real?" with "What exactly would I need to see to be persuaded?" and "If not literal, what encoded memory or technique might this legend preserve?"

Part A — Atlas of the Beneath: A Conversational Map of Global Subterranean Legends & Alleged Sites

This is not a gazetteer of every hole and rumor; it's a guided walk where the stories cluster and the ground, quite often, answers back. Read each region as an invitation. Under every stop, you'll find "Notebooks" to turn passive reading into active inquiry.

1) Anatolia & the Near East — Cities Under Ash and Tuff

Volcanic tuff in central Anatolia carves like bread and holds like bone. Multilevel underground towns—with ventilation shafts, stables, kitchens, chapels, storage rooms, and rolling-stone doors—sit beneath surface settlements like cooler second cities. Legends speak of people who "went under" to survive winter, raids, or drought; ritual traditions point to darkness and silence as curriculum rather than punishment.

Notebook prompts

- Which local terms are applied—*city, shelter, sanctuary*—and what do those words imply about function?

_____

_____

_____

_____

_____

- In cross-section sketches, where do you see planned intersections (air shafts crossing gathering halls)? Why there?

_____

_____

_____

_____

_____

- If a tale says "only the worthy can open the door," what simple mechanism (counterweights, smoke-draft, latch) or social rule (password, vow, lineage) might be dramatized?

- What traces of long underground life would you expect—soot patterns, cooking residues, reused water channels? Record your predictions before you check reports.

2) The Levant & Mesopotamia — Gates, Wells, and the River Below

Here, the ground is a palimpsest of *tells* and under-architectures: cisterns, qanats, drains, tombs, and processional passages. Myth speaks of judges, gates, oaths, and river crossings; the soil replies with measured hydraulics and repeatable rites. Your job is to map the bureaucracy of the underworld against the bureaucracy of water.

Notebook prompts

- List water-control features (cisterns, channels, overflow sumps). What rites would naturally grow around them?

_____

_____

_____

_____

_____

_____

_____

_____

_____

- Where do underground routes allow controlled appearance/disappearance—liturgical theater doubling as civic power?

_____

_____

_____

_____

_____

_____

_____

_____

_____

3) Caucasus & Inner Asia — Thresholds, Winds, and Rumors of Networks

Across the Caucasus and through Inner Asia, mountain hearts hide grottoes and passways. Esoteric narratives speak of hidden polities—subterranean sanctuaries linked by natural cavities and disciplined access, not planet-sized voids. Treat the idea less as "global hollow" and more as a distributed refuge ecology: many small nodes, selectively permeable.

Notebook prompts

- Overlay place-names for "snake/dragon," "gate," "jewel," and "wind-door" with karst belts and old lava fields; note convergences.

_____

_____

_____

_____

_____

_____

_____

_____

_____

- Interview custodians for non-spectacular details (e.g., "the ridge breathes in winter"), not only the big legends.

4) South Asia — Pātāla, Nāga-Realms, and the Cave as Laboratory

Indic cosmology stacks worlds; the "below" is not merely punitive. Nāga-lore, cave yogic traditions, and engineered retreats present the underground as a laboratory—a controlled environment for transforming attention. Discern moral allegory from logistics—and note where they overlap.

Notebook prompts

- Catalog cave monasteries or meditation cells near springs. What acoustics and temperatures do they exploit?

_____

_____

_____

_____

_____

_____

_____

_____

- Track serpent/river motifs: do they encode flood behavior or irrigation calendars?

_____

_____

_____

_____

_____

_____

_____

_____

_____

5) The Himalaya & Plateau — Shambhala as Operating System, Places as Hardware

Read Shambhala two ways at once: a dharmic social design (the OS) and, occasionally, addressable sanctuaries (the hardware) where that OS can run at high fidelity. Access isn't a map; it's a practice. That dual reading keeps wonder intact while protecting the method.

Notebook prompts

- For a "hidden valley," log weather peculiarities, wind walls, and cloud rings. Could these create isolation pockets that incidentally protect lineages and archives?

_____

_____

_____

_____

_____

_____

_____

- Separate pedagogy from pageantry: what behaviors are trained by the journey?

_____

_____

_____

_____

_____

_____

_____

_____

6) East Asia — Grotto-Heavens and Mountain Cosmograms

Daoist grotto-heavens (*dongtian*) present cave-mountains as cosmograms: threshold places where internal alchemy is trained and landscapes behave like mandalas. Map ritual routes, echo-nodes, and "soul-holes" against star lore and seasonal winds.

Notebook prompts

- Chart cave "addresses" in mandala terms: outer court, inner hall, secret chamber.

_____

_____

_____

_____

_____

_____

_____

- Do seasonal festivals coincide with light strikes or airflow inversions?

_____

_____

_____

_____

_____

_____

_____

_____

_____

_____

7) Europe — Hades, Sídhe, and Catacomb Pedagogies

Greek, Celtic, and later Christian undergrounds differ in doctrine but share choreography: gates and guardians; rules about food and looking; initiation modeled as death-and-return. Treat catacombs and barrows as classrooms, not just repositories.

Notebook prompts

- If a mound is "a door," what legal and ritual structures surround it (taboos, hospitality, oaths)?

_____

_____

_____

_____

_____

_____

_____

- Match mythic rules to architectural features (e.g., single-file spirals that enforce silence).

_____

_____

_____

_____

_____

_____

_____

8) North Africa & the Nile — Duat Underfoot, Processions in Stone

Texts stage the sun's nightly passage through a tiered Duat; tomb complexes enact the sequence with chambers, wells, and under-corridors. Follow the water and the light, not only the titles on the wall.

Notebook prompts

- Note shafts that breathe (drafts) and wells that "speak" (resonance). Could these be the practical correlates of underworld scenes?

_____

_____

_____

_____

_____

_____

_____

_____

_____

_____

9) The Americas — Xibalba Gates, Sipapuni, and the Long Karst

From Mesoamerican cave rites to the Hopi's emergence places, the continent's limestone and volcanic formations host a choreography of trials, offerings, and origin claims. Treat popular newspaper legends (e.g., "lost subterranean cities" in dramatic canyons) with curiosity and method: romance is not record.

Notebook prompts

- In watery caves, log "House of Cold/Razor/Jaguar/Bats" correlates: frigid pools, knife-sharp breakdown, predator roosts.

- For emergence sites, begin with stewards' voices; map policy closures as contours of care, not conspiracies.

10) Oceania & Volcanic Arcs — Lava Tubes and Ancestral Corridors

Basaltic fields gift smooth, elongated tubes with skylights—excellent refuges and ritual theaters when airflow is managed and water condenses reliably. Read stories of "people under the mountain" with a lava-tube map in hand.

Notebook prompts

- Track skylight spacing and prevailing winds: where are the natural bellows?

_____

_____

_____

_____

_____

_____

_____

_____

_____

- Record condensation points and traditional use (rest, storage, rites) along the route.

11) Global Signatures — Where the Ground Itself Whispers "Look Here"

Twelve Places Most Likely to Hide a Cache (pin these on your working   map)
Sealed karst chambers; lava tubes; talus-sealed shelters; avulsed river terraces; sub-floor temple voids; backfilled enclosures; abandoned aqueduct galleries; salt caves; permafrost bluffs; bog margins; scree-masked cliff alcoves; repurposed mine adits.

Part B — Reflection Prompts: Choosing Your Compelling Underground Myth

Use these to turn attraction into analysis. Pick one myth or site and walk through these questions slowly.

1. **First pull.** Why did this story choose you—landscape, guardian figure, promise of a gift? Note the exact image or sentence that hooked you. (No polishing; write the messy truth.)

_____

_____

_____

_____

_____

_____

_____

_____

_____

2. **Four-layer lens.** For your chosen myth, identify:
   • Practical layer (shelter, water, defense).
   • Ritual layer (sound, light, procession).
   • Cosmological layer (tiers, guardians, trials).
   • Memory layer (encoded disaster, taboo, survival tactic).

_____

_____

_____

_____

_____

_____

_____

_____

_____

_____

_____

_____

_____

3. **Guide/Gate/Gift.** Who is the guide? Where is the gate? What
   returns with the explorer (law, song, calendar, seed)? Sketch a
   minimal storyboard.

_____

_____

_____

_____

_____

4. **Two truths test.** What parts work beautifully as teacher-myth? What parts fail as geology or logistics? Keep both truths on the table.

_____

_____

_____

_____

_____

_____

_____

_____

5. **The knowledge filter.** If this myth were inconvenient to a reigning model, where might it get sidelined—language labels

("ritual object"), access control, career risk? Note how you'd test past the filter without throwing rigor away.

_____

_____

_____

_____

_____

_____

_____

_____

_____

6. **Your ethics.** Who holds guardianship over the place/story now? What permissions would you need? What should remain unpublished? Write a consent plan first.

_____

_____

_____

_____

_____

_____

_____

_____

_____

7. **Prediction engine.** Draft one prediction your reading makes ("a solstice light-strike should hit this carving," "there should be a hidden drain beneath the 'serpent' hall"). A good myth reading generates a field test.

_____

_____

_____

_____

_____

_____

_____

_____

_____

8. **Behavioral yield.** If you truly believed this myth's *teaching*, what would you do differently tomorrow? (Underworld stories are operational protocols, not just beliefs.)

Part C — Research Checklist: Exploring Myths Critically Without Losing Wonder

Tape this to the inside cover of your field notebook. It's a practical protocol—salvageable wonder paired with hard checks.

1) Build a Map That Predicts

- **Toponymy sweep:** Collect place-names for "gate," "snake/dragon," "wind," "hidden," "well," "city of stone."

Prioritize clusters near karst belts, basaltic fields, and old river terraces.

- **Geomorphology pass:** Mark dolines, sinkholes, resurgences, poljes, and talus fans. Caches prefer edges.

- **Hydrology spine:** Where water disappears and reappears, people negotiate. That's where rites grow.

2) Choose the Right Instruments (Non-Destructive First)

- **LiDAR** to strip the canopy and find surface grids.

- **GPR/ERT** to separate geology from architecture.

- **Magnetometry/gradiometry** to catch fired features and subtle ditch/wall signatures.

- **Muon radiography/microtremor** for voids inside big masses.

- **Photogrammetry/RTI** to read faint inscriptions and plan models.

Pair tools; let one aim the next.

3) Run the Myth Through the Four-Layer Filter

- Practical • Ritual • Cosmological • Memory.

- Ask where elites reframed older practices to consolidate power.

4) Set Safety & Ethics Before Curiosity

- Never enter caves without qualified local guides, permits, and proper equipment.

- The underground is a consent-only space. Always have a "thread"—guide, time limit, return plan.

- Protect coordinates if disclosure invites looting or desecration.

5) Anticipate the Knowledge Filter

- Expect labels like "ritual object" to be used prematurely; ask what data would move an object to a different category.

- Recognize site control and career pressures; build collaborations that diffuse risk while raising rigor.

6) Separate Romance From Record (Without Killing Either)

- **Romance** motivates hypotheses and preserves memory.

- **Record** accepts or rejects mechanisms.

- Keep both by aiming romance at testable predictions and letting the record revise the narrative.

7) Write Up Like a Steward, Not a Conqueror

- Distinguish measured, inferred, and imagined.

- Name uncertainties.

- Share credit with local knowledge keepers.

- Publish enough context to be useful; withhold enough detail to be protective where appropriate.

Part D — Resource Library: Texts, Documentaries, and Field Reports (Use With Discernment)

This section is a *framework* for curating your library in a way that preserves wonder and improves signal. It's intentionally author-neutral here; you'll populate it with vetted sources that fit your project and ethics.

1) Texts (Foundational & Comparative)

What belongs here

- Regional cave archaeology syntheses; ritual architecture studies; hydrology & geoarchaeology references; cross-cultural analyses of descent motifs.

- Manuals on non-destructive survey (LiDAR, GPR, magnetometry) and field acoustics.

How to vet quickly

- Is the argument falsifiable (does it predict where to look/what to measure)?

- Does it distinguish myth's teaching function from geology's constraints (two-truths discipline)?

Notebook fields to complete for each text

- Core claim in one sentence: _____

- Evidence type (material / textual/ethnographic/instrumental): _____

- Predicted test I can run: _____

- Stewardship concerns raised: _____

2) Documentaries (Visual Ethnography & Sites)

What belongs here

- Films that show *process*: permissions sought, methods used, negative results included, and living community voices foregrounded.

- Pieces that demonstrate the ethics of "partner, not prize."

Red flags

- Single-source sensational claims; blurred chains of custody; "suppressed diary" hooks without provenance. (Enjoy as folklore; do not file as data.)

Notebook fields

- Who speaks (stewards/scientists/storytellers)?
  _____

- What's measured versus dramatized?
  _____

- One practice I learned to adopt:
  _____

3) Field Reports (Site-Level, Method-Forward)

What belongs here

- Survey reports that pair geophysics with limited, respectful test excavations.

- Papers that log airflow, light-strike calendars, hydrology behavior, and acoustic profiles—*the nuts and bolts of underground life.*

Quick triage

- Are the instruments the right ones for the geology?

- Are raw or summarized datasets available for re-analysis?

- Does the report explain what was *not* found as clearly as what was?

Notebook fields

- Geological context (karst, basalt, talus, salt): _____

- Preservation profile (organics/metals/ceramics likely?): _____

- Access notes & ethics: _____

Tear-Out Worksheets (Copy for Your Notebook)

Worksheet 1 — Myth-to-Method Converter

Myth/Legend chosen: _____
Hook image/sentence: _____
Guide / Gate / Gift: _____ / _____ / _____
Four layers (practical / ritual / cosmological / memory):
• _____ • _____ • _____ • _____
Prediction the reading makes (testable): _____
Instrument(s) to test it (LiDAR/GPR/...): _____
Stewardship & permissions plan: _____

Worksheet 2 — Site Walk (Plan + Section)

Entrance geometry: _____
Light behavior (dates/times): _____
Airflow (drafts, breathing points): _____
Hydrology (pools, resurgences): _____
Acoustic notes (clap test, bloom notes): _____
Hazards/egress (two exits?): _____
What not to publish (protective redactions): _____

Worksheet 3 — "From Claim to Check"

Claim (verbatim): _____
Provenance (chain of custody): _____
Hard-data crosschecks (seismic/gravity/heat flow): _____
Symbol salvage (if mechanism fails, what teaching remains?):
_____
Outcome: accept/revise / archive as folklore (circle one)

Field Mini-Guides

A) Acoustic Sense-Making Underground

Low volume hums, hand drums, and call-and-response reveal where a chamber "chooses" notes. Mark resonant nodes on your plan; correlate with soot or polish on stone where people likely stood. (Ritual standardization often leaves acoustic fingerprints.)

B) Hydrology as Ritual Spine

Threshold pools, clean re-emergences, and seasonal inversions ("backward rivers") generate predictable rites: purification, offerings, timing. Map water first; story often follows.

C) Preservation Logic (What Survives Where)

Karst with stable humidity preserves organics episodically; salt caves can "pickle" fibers; permafrost and bog margins hold delicate materials; basalt tubes are friendly to architecture but less to paper. Predict finds before you dig; let the environment set your expectations.

Quick Debates (And How to Stay Sane Inside Them)

- "It's all suppressed!"

Sometimes gatekeeping is real; sometimes the data just aren't there yet. Demand rigor from orthodoxy and dissent alike; don't let "suppressed" be the magic word that turns fiction into fact.

- "Prove the literal city or shut up."

False choice. Salvage the teaching even if the mechanism fails; then aim for modest, testable claims (a drain, a light-strike, a vault), not megastructures.

- "Ritual = meaningless."

Backward. Ritual is dense code. Decode the choreography—light, sound, water—before you file it under "mystery."

Capstone Exercise — Build Your Own "Explorer's Ledger"

Create a facing-page spread: left page for legend motifs (serpent, twin pillars, river), right page for site data (rock type, water table, orientation, access notes). Every time the two pages rhyme, draw a thread—and plan a test.

Pack Your Light

We end where we began: hand on cold wall, breath slowed, both lamps lit. This workbook is not a trophy case; it's a method. Treat myths as serious hypotheses about what people noticed when noticing could save them. Treat underground places as partners, not prizes. Move toward the extraordinary by doing the ordinary work extraordinarily well. Then go see where the old stories touch the ground.

Conclusion

We set out with two lamps—wonder and method—and we have tried to keep them lit together. That pairing is the spine of this book: to meet the worlds oldest descent stories with curiosity that doesn't flinch and with tests that don't sneer. "Keep both lamps lit," we said at the threshold; it remains the instruction at the exit.

Across four parts, a pattern held. First, we listened to the grand claims—hollow worlds, hidden kingdoms, shining cities below—and read them as modern echoes of an older grammar of descent: Gate, Guide, Gift. Then we walked real stone—Cappadocia's cities, labyrinths under temples, the ritual caves where darkness and sound do their precise work. We examined how gatekeeping and "knowledge filters" shape what is seen, said, and funded. Finally, we braided myth, mind, and measurement, testing legends against geology, acoustics, hydrology, and the stubborn physiologies of bodies in the dark.

What endures from that braid is simple and serious:

- The underworld is real—as ritual, as psychology, and as archaeology. It has taught us for millennia.

- A mechanical "hollow planet" remains a mirror more than a map—powerful as metaphor, thin as measurement.

Why it matters is equally direct: cultures used underground places to store their best pattern recognition—about sky, water, risk, seasons, and how to live together when the world tilts. When we learn to read those caches without romance or contempt, we recover instructions, not fantasies.

What We Carry Out

A method. Keep a double ledger: legend on the left, measurements on the right. Mark the rhymes—serpents, birds, rivers, twin pillars—and then ask where the rock, the light, and the water agree. When the pages line up, plan a test.

A map. Read any descent through four layers at once: practical (shelter, water, defense), ritual (sound, light, procession), cosmological (tiers, guardians, trials), and memory (taboo, catastrophe, survival code). And keep watching for the core triad—Guide, Gate, Gift—because it tells you who leads, how you cross, and what must return with you.

A toolbox. We now have instruments that make the ground more transparent—LiDAR, GPR, muon radiography, hyperspectral imaging, and computational acoustics. Use them to salvage what can be salvaged and to replace certainty's swagger with testable claims. Start small: a drain, a light-strike, a vault.

A stance. Model a better debate: demand provenance before belief, and hard data crosschecks before dismissal. Salvage the symbol when the mechanism fails. Refuse the false choice between awe and evidence.

A citizenship. You do not need a grant to contribute. Walk fields after rain. Listen for old place-names that mean gate, well, or city of stone. Map with your phone. Partner with custodians who hold keys no satellite can see. Respect is not sentiment—it is methodology.

An ethic. Consent first, minimal intrusion, publication as restitution, and reburial when asked. "Finding" is not winning. We are guests where others keep shrines and ancestors. Leave places able to keep their secrets if they choose.

What Still Calls From Below

Some questions are now pointed enough to be useful. What is the true extent of underground habitation around famous sites and into their quiet hinterlands? Which acoustic signatures betray deliberate tuning for chant or trance? How do hidden waterworks encode calendars and risk management? Where do sealed spaces align with living taboos—and why? These are no longer slogans; they are project briefs—each one testable, each one worth the humility of a null result.

And some invitations remain deliberately wider. Read the descent as technology: a designed sequence of thresholds that stresses the senses just enough to produce vision, then binds that vision to ethics on return. Read the same sequence as a civic machine: a way to rehearse grief, courage, and cooperation until a community can survive its winters together. These readings don't cancel the possibility of "others" encountered at depth; they simply remind us that transformation is the common denominator.

A Last Word to the Explorer

If this book has done its work, you leave with both lamps still lit. You know now to test before you trumpet, to listen before you label, to ask the land and its keepers what they already know. You have seen how often myth behaves like a micro-manual—two exits, a backward river, a guardian animal that is also a season or a draft of air—and how often those notes become survival when the sky misbehaves.

You have also seen that the point of going down is not to hoard a story, but to return with a gift—law, song, seed, technique—and to pay for it with service. The underworld is not a warehouse for the dead; it is a school for the living. The test is not whether it "really happened," but whether you live differently when you come back.

So here is our closing pledge, revised by the journey:

- We will treat myths as serious hypotheses about what people noticed when noticing could save them.

- We will treat underground places as partners, not prizes.

- We will move toward the extraordinary only by way of the ordinary work the extraordinary requires.

Hand on the cool wall, breath slowed, the light ahead brightens. Step through—boots muddy, notes in your pocket, questions sharpened— and go look where the old stories touch the ground. The realms below are not just where the dead go. They are where the living learn how to begin again.

www.ingramcontent.com/pod-product-compliance
Lightning Source LLC
Chambersburg PA
CBHW060739050426
42449CB00008B/1270